# CATALOGUE OF
# SMALL-SCALE FISHING GEAR

## CATALOGUE DES
## *ENGINS DE PECHE ARTISANALE*

## CATALOGO DE
## ARTES DE PESCA ARTESANAL

**Edited by**
*Edité par*
Editado por

**C. Nédélec**
**Fishery Industries Division, FAO**

*Division des industries de la pêche, FAO*

Dirección de Industrias Pesqueras, FAO

Published by arrangement with the Food and Agriculture Organization of the United Nations
by Fishing News (Books) Ltd., 23 Rosemount Avenue, West Byfleet, Surrey, England.

ISBN 0 85238 077 1

Printed in Great Britain by
The Whitefriars Press Ltd., London and Tonbridge

# Contents
## *Sommaire*
## Indice

# I Foreword
## *Avant-propos*
## Prólogo

This edition of the FAO Catalogue of Fishing Gear Designs deals especially with small-scale fisheries using gears operated from the shore or from small boats in coastal or inland waters. Maximum size of fishing vessels included in this catalogue is approximately 15 m length overall, with an engine power of not more than 150 h.p.

For the categories of gear concerned, the type, shape and materials, as well as the operational methods, usually vary considerably. It is therefore impossible to cover in a single work all the numerous possible variations of the different fishing methods. It should, in fact, be noted that this catalogue is by no means an exhaustive list of all existing types of fishing gear; it merely covers a limited, though quite representative, selection of the main types of gear that have proved profitable in commercial fisheries. We would point out that, in order to keep our selection within reasonable limits, we have on the whole confined our descriptions to gear made from conventional materials, i.e. nets, ropes and lines, whereas miscellaneous gear such as harpoons, grappling tools and harvesting machines, as well as gear made from unconventional materials such as boughs, bamboo, rattan, etc., have been excluded because their local variations are too numerous.

It is nevertheless hoped that this fairly wide range will enable users to select more efficient gears, adapting them where necessary to the fishing conditions usually encountered. Furthermore, because of the different sources of gear, used in both developed and developing countries, the reader will find new ideas or general principles here, on the basis of which he will improve or adapt his own traditional gear.

*La présente édition du Catalogue FAO de dessins d'engins de pêche est plus particulièrement consacrée aux pêches; artisanales, effectuées avec des engins utilisés du rivage ou à bord de petites embarcations dans les eaux côtières maritimes ou dans les eaux continentales. La taille limite des bateaux de pêche qui ont été retenus pour ce catalogue est d'environ 15 m de longueur hors-tout, avec une force motrice maximale de 150 ch.*

*Dans les catégories des engins concernés on constate généralement une extrême variété de types et de formes, ainsi que de matériaux constitutifs et de méthodes d'utilisation. Il était donc impossible de représenter dans le même ouvrage toutes les nombreuses variations possibles des différentes méthodes de pêche. En fait, il convient de souligner que ce catalogue ne constitue pas un répertoire complet de tous les engins de pêche existants; il groupe seulement un choix limité, bien que assez représentatif, des principaux engins de pêche qui se sont révélés fructueux en utilisation commerciale. Nous devons préciser aussi que, pour cette même raison de maintenir notre sélection dans des limites raisonnables, nous n'avons retenu en général que les descriptions d'engins fabriqués à partir des matériaux conventionnels, à savoir: filets, cordages et lignes, tandis que les engins divers comme les harpons, les outils de ramassage et les machines à récolter, ainsi que les engins constitués par des matériaux non conventionnels, tels que branchages, bambous, rotin, n'ont pas été retenus en raison notamment de leurs trop nombreuses variations locales.*

*On espère néanmoins que cette gamme suffisamment étendue permettra aux utilisateurs de choisir des engins de pêche plus efficaces, sous réserve de les adapter*

Esta edición del Catálogo de la FAO de planos de aparejos de pesca está dedicada ante todo al equipo utilizado para la pesca artesanal en aguas marítimas o continentales desde la costa misma o a bordo de pequeñas embarcaciones. Para la inclusión de embarcaciones de pesca en este catálogo se ha tomado como límite máximo una eslora total de 15 m aproximadamente, con una fuerza motriz máxima de 150 h.p.

Los aparejos de que aquí se trata existen en una enorme variedad de tipos, formas y materiales y también los métodos de empleo son muy diversos. Ha resultado, pues, imposible, incluir en una misma obra todas las variaciones posibles. Conviene subrayar, por tanto, que este catálogo no constituye un repertorio completo de todo el equipo existente de pesca; se ha escogido solamente una gama limitada, aunque bastante representativa, de los aparejos que han dado buenos resultados en la pesca comercial. Hemos de precisar también que, a fin de mantener nuestra selección dentro de límites razonables, no hemos incluido en general más que la descripción del equipo fabricado con los materiales usuales: redes, cabos y líneas, mientras que los aparejos diversos como los arpones, los utensilios de recolección y las máquinas de recogida así como los aparejos hechos de otros materiales como ramajes, bambú, bejuco, etc., no se han incluido por ser excesivo el número de variedades locales.

Es de esperar, sin embargo, que la gama que aquí se presenta, suficientemente amplia, permita a los usuarios escoger el equipo de pesca más eficaz, adaptándolo eventualmente a sus condiciones habituales de pesca. Por otro lado, dada la diversa proveniencia de los aparejos que se utilizan tanto en países desarrollados como en países en desarrollo, es probable que el usuario encuentre ideas nuevas o principios

This catalogue is in fact intended primarily for professional fishermen, netmakers or manufacturers of other fishing gear, for teachers in fishery schools or training centres, and for fishery extension workers. Officers responsible for fisheries administration and regulation will also find useful information and reference data here.

As in the previous catalogues, especially to overcome language barriers, the text has been kept to an absolute minimum. However, unlike the preceding volumes, with a view to being particularly useful to developing fisheries, more emphasis has been placed on the practical construction of gear and especially on its operation, in particular by the use of sketches or photographs showing the layout and fishing auxiliaries of the boat as well as the successive stages of its manoeuvring and the handling of gear during fishing.

Apart from the usual references to the international standards of the International Organization for Standardization (ISO), particularly with regard to textile materials and to drawings of nets (e.g. tex-system, hanging ratio and cutting rate), the International Standard Classification for Fishing Gear, as adopted by the International Council for the Exploration of the Sea (ICES), the International Commission for Northwest Atlantic Fisheries (ICNAF) and other international bodies, has been followed for the general plan and the terminology of the catalogue.

This catalogue has been prepared by the Fish Production and Marketing Service, Fishery Industries Division of the FAO Department of Fisheries. We are particularly grateful to the fishermen, net manufacturers, commercial fishing companies, fishing technologists and masterfishermen who supplied the necessary data for the preparation of the descriptions of fishing gear. Without their help it would not have been possible to publish this catalogue. Moreover, our thanks are expressed to Prof. A. von Brandt (Hamburg, Federal Republic of Germany) who, in addition to his numerous contributions, has kindly given us his competent advice, as well as to the consultants, Mr. P. Y. Dremière (Sea Fisheries Institute, Sète, France) and Mr. M. Kaulin (Maikammer, Federal Republic of Germany) for their assistance in the preparation of most of the designs. Finally, we thank Miss A. Barcali and Mr. M. Carlesi, draftsmen of the FAO Department of Fisheries, for the

éventuellement à leurs conditions de pêche habituelles. D'autre part, en raison même de la provenance diverse des engins, utilisés tant dans les pays développés que dans les pays en développement, l'utilisateur trouvera ici les idées nouvelles ou les principes généraux qui doivent lui permettre d'améliorer ou d'ajuster ses propres engins de pêche traditionnels.

Ce catalogue est donc destiné en premier lieu aux pêcheurs professionnels, aux fabricants de filets ou autres engins de pêche, ainsi qu'aux instructeurs des écoles de pêche ou centres de formation et aux vulgarisateurs sur le terrain. Le personnel chargé de l'administration et de la réglementation des pêches y trouvera lui aussi des informations utiles et des données de référence.

Comme pour les précédents catalogues, et en particulier pour éviter le problème des langues, le rôle du texte a été réduit au plus strict minimum. Toutefois, à la différence des volumes déjà publiés, et dans le but d'être particulièrement utile aux pêcheries en développement, on a porté davantage l'accent sur la construction pratique de l'engin et surtout sur son mode d'utilisation, notamment à l'aide de schémas ou de photographies montrant l'agencement du bateau et de ses accessoires de pêche, ainsi que les phases successives des manoeuvres en pêche.

Indépendamment des références habituelles aux normes internationales préparées par l'ISO (Organisation internationale de normalisation), notamment pour ce qui est des matériaux textiles et de la représentation des filets (par exemple: système tex, taux d'armement et processus de coupe), on a suivi, pour le plan général du catalogue et pour la terminologie, la Classification internationale type des engins de pêche, telle qu'elle est maintenant adoptée par le CIEM (Conseil international pour l'exploration de la mer), l'ICNAF (Commission internationale des pêcheries du Nord-ouest Atlantique) et autres organismes internationaux.

Le catalogue a été préparé dans le Service de la production et de la commercialisation du poisson, Division des industries de la pêche, au Département des pêches de la FAO. Nous tenons à remercier les pêcheurs professionnels, les fabricants de filets, les sociétés commerciales de pêche et les experts technologistes des pêches et maîtres-pêcheurs, qui nous ont fourni les données nécessaires à la préparation des descriptions d'engins de pêche. Sans leur contribution, ce travail n'aurait pu être mené à bien. Par ailleurs, nous remercions tout particulièrement le

generales que le permitan mejorar o ajustar su equipo tradicional de pesca.

Este catálogo está destinado, pues, ante todo a los pescadores profesionales, a los fabricantes de redes u otros aparejos de pesca, a los profesores de escuelas o centros de formación pesquera y a los divulgadores. También el personal responsable de la administración y regulación de la pesca encontrará informaciones útiles y puntos de referencia.

Igual que en catálogos anteriores, se ha reducido el texto al mínimo, para evitar el problema de la diferencia de idiomas. Sin embargo, a diferencia de los volúmenes ya publicados, y para que el catálogo sea especialmente útil a las pesquerías en desarrollo, se ha insistido más en la construcción práctica del equipo y en la forma de utilizarlo, sirviéndose para ello de esquemas o fotografías que muestran la disposición de la embarcación y de sus accesorios de pesca y las fases sucesivas de la maniobra.

Además de las referencias habituales a las normas internacionales preparadas por la ISO (Organización Internacional de Unificación de Normas), sobre todo por lo que se refiere a los materiales textiles y la representación de las redes (por ejemplo, coeficientes de armadura y tipo de corte de los paños), para el plano general del catálogo y la terminología se ha utilizado la clasificación internacional uniforme de aparejos de pesca adoptada por el CIEM (Consejo Internacional para la Exploración del Mar), la CIPAN o ICNAF (Comisión Internacional de Pesquerías del Atlántico Noroeste) y otros organismos internacionales.

El catálogo ha sido preparado por el Servicio de Producción y Mercadeo Pesqueros (Dirección de Industrias Pesqueras) del Departamento de Pesca de la FAO. Deseamos expresar nuestro agradecimiento a los pescadores profesionales, fabricantes de redes, sociedades comerciales, expertos, tecnólogos y patrones de pesca que nos han facilitado los datos necesarios para preparar las descripciones de los aparejos. Sin su contribución hubiera sido imposible llevar a término este trabajo. Gracias especiales merecen el Prof. A. von Brandt (Hamburgo, República Federal de Alemania) que, además de sus numerosas contribuciones nos ha graciosamente dado sus preciosos consejos, así como los consultores, Sres. P. Y. Dremière (Institut des pêches maritimes, Sète, Francia) y M. Kaulin (Maikammer, República Federal de Alemania), que nos han ayudado a preparar la mayoría de los planos. Por último, hemos de dar las gracias a la Sra. A. Barcali y al Sr. M. Carlesi,

presentation and final composition of the gear descriptive plates.

professeur A. von Brandt (Hambourg, République fédérale d'Allemagne), qui en plus de ses nombreuses contributions nous a aimablement donné son avis compétent, ainsi que les experts-conseils M. P. Y. Dremière (Institut des pêches maritimes, Sète, France) et M. M. Kaulin (Maikammer, République fédérale d'Allemagne), qui nous ont apporté leur aide pour la préparation de la plupart des plans. Enfin, nos remerciements s'adressent également à Mlle A. Barcali et M. M. Carlesi, dessinateurs du Département des pêches de la FAO, pour la présentation et la composition finales des planches descriptives des engins.

dibujantes del Departamento de Pesca de la FAO, por la presentación y composición final de las láminas descriptivas.

# II Mode of Presentation
## *Mode de présentation*
## Presentación

Indispensable text is given in the three working languages of FAO, i.e. English, French and Spanish. All information is included in the drawing. Abbreviations and symbols (Appendix 1) have been selected so as to be as self-explanatory as possible.

So far as possible the main design drawings are to scale and the scale is then indicated in metric equivalents. For obvious reasons this scale cannot refer to both netting and framing lines. To overcome this, basic *drawing rules* had to be adopted.

*Surrounding nets* (purse seines, lamparas, etc.). The length (horizontal) is drawn according to the length of the floatline and the depth (vertical) according to the fully stretched netting.
*Trawls.* The width of netting panels or sections is drawn according to half the stretched netting and the depth or length according to the fully stretched netting.
*Gillnets, tangle nets.* The length is drawn according to the length of the floatline. When the net has side lines the depth is drawn according to their length. The depth of nets without side lines is shown according to the fully stretched netting.

*Other gear* (dredges, pots, lines, etc.). In view of the great variety in construction and the limited number of designs of the different other gear types a standardization of presentation would be impractical. Schematic or partly perspective overall sketches complemented by detail drawings according to requirements are considered preferable at this stage to provide self-explanatory specifications. Dimensions are given and scales indicated where applicable.

*Les indications indispensables sont fournies dans les trois langues de travail de la FAO, c'est-à-dire l'anglais, le français et l'espagnol. Toutes les données sont portées sur les plans mêmes. Les abréviations et symboles (cf. annexe 1) ont été choisis de manière à être aussi compréhensibles que possible.*

*Dans la mesure du possible, les principaux plans sont à l'échelle et celle-ci est alors indiquée en équivalent métrique. Cette échelle ne pouvant évidemment s'appliquer à la fois aux filets et aux ralingues, il a fallu adopter certaines conventions de dessin fondamentales.*

Filets tournants *(sennes coulissantes, lamparas, etc.). La longueur (horizontale) est dessinée suivant la longueur de la ralingue des flotteurs et la profondeur (verticale) suivant la longueur de l'alèze étirée.*
Chaluts. *La largeur des pièces ou sections correspond à la moitié de la largeur de l'alèze étirée et leur profondeur ou longueur correspond à la longueur de l'alèze étirée.*
Filets maillants et dérivants. *La longueur est dessinée suivant la longueur de la ralingue des flotteurs. Lorsque le filet a des ralingues latérales, la profondeur est dessinée suivant leur longueur. La profondeur des filets dépourvus de ralingues latérales est indiquée suivant la longueur de l'alèze étirée.*

Autres engins *(dragues, casiers, lignes, etc.). Etant donné la grande variété des modes de construction et le nombre limité de dessins des divers autres types d'engins, une normalisation de la présentation serait irréalisable. A ce stade, on a jugé préférable de donner des dessins schématiques ou des dessins en semi-perspective, complétés par des plans détaillés selon les besoins, afin de fournir des spécifications compréhensibles. Lorsque cela était possible, on a indiqué les dimensions et l'échelle.*

El texto indispensable aparece en los tres idiomas de trabajo de la FAO: español, francés e inglés. Toda la información va incluida en el plano. Se emplean abreviaturas y símbolos (Apéndice 1) seleccionados de modo que resulten lo más explícitos posible.

En cuanto ha sido posible, las formas principales se han trazado a escala, que se indica en el sistema métrico. Por razones fáciles de comprender esta escala no se puede aplicar a los paños y a las relingas de contorno simultáneamente. Para vencer este problema se tuvieron que adoptar *reglas de dibujo* fundamentales.

*Redes de cerco* (de jareta, lamparos, etc.). La longitud (horizontal) corresponde a la de la relinga de flotadores y la altura (vertical) a los paños totalmente estirados.
*Artes de arrastre.* La anchura de los paños o secciones corresponde a la mitad de la malla estirada y la altura o longitud a la malla totalmente estirada.
*Redes de enmalle, trasmallo.* La longitud corresponde a la de la relinga de flotadores. Si tienen relingas laterales, la altura corresponde a su longitud. La altura de las redes sin relingas laterales corresponde a los paños totalmente estirados.

*Otro equipo* (almadrabas, biturones, nasas, líneas, etc.). Dada su enorme variedad y los pocos planos de los diferentes tipos, no sería práctico presentarlos de manera uniforme. En estos momentos es preferible hacer dibujos globales en perspectiva o esquemáticos complementados por otros detallados, según las necesidades, para ofrecer características de fácil comprensión. Se dan las dimensiones y se indican las escalas.

No están a escala la mayor parte de los esbozos generales, por ejemplo: del

General outline drawings, e.g., of the rig of a complete gear, which are meant to facilitate the understanding, as well as detail drawings of components, are mostly not to scale. Instead, essential dimensions are given. Materials are indicated (abbreviations, Appendix 1) only when considered necessary.

Of the metric system, which has been adopted throughout for *dimensions,* only the units metre (m) and millimetre (mm) are utilized. Equivalents in the Anglo-American system are given in Appendix 2. In order to avoid over-crowding of the drawings the units are sometimes omitted. They can, however, always be recognized from the context and the mode of presentation. The metre is used for larger dimensions such as lengths of footropes, headlines, floatlines, bridles and applies to figures having a point followed by two decimals (e.g., 5.25; 90.20). The millimetre is used for smaller dimensions such as meshsize (stretched), diameters of ropes, floats or bobbins and in the detail drawings. It applies to the figures without a point (e.g., 12; 527; 2305), or with one decimal only (e.g., 1.2).

The unit for *mass* and *weight* is the kilogramme (kg). Forces such as breaking load of netting yarns or ropes and buoyancies of floats are given in kilogramme-force (kgf) or gramme-force (gf) which, because of their relation with kg or g are considered more convenient for the reader than the unit newton (N) adopted by the International System of Units (1 kgf=9.8 N). Equivalents in the Anglo-American system are also given in Appendix 2.

*Materials* are indicated by abbreviations which are preferably based on terms in common international use, such as plastic (PL), sisal (SIS), polyamide (PA). They are listed in Appendix 1. A rather comprehensive tabulation of trade names of synthetic materials used in fishing gear, arranged according to the main chemical groups, is presented in Appendix 3.

The *size of netting yarns* is designated according to the tex system and R-tex was adopted as the only unit because of its general applicability. It indicates the "resultant linear density" of the finished netting yarn by its weight in grammes per one thousand metres. For monofilament also the diameter in millimetres is given. This serves at the same time to indicate monofilament as compared with twisted or braided netting yarns. Formulas and tabulations for conversion into some

*Les esquisses générales, c'est-à-dire celles qui donnent le gréement d'un engin complet, dont l'objet est de faciliter la compréhension du lecteur, de même que les plans détaillés des parties constitutives, ne sont généralement pas à l'échelle. En revanche, les dimensions essentielles sont données. Les matériaux ne sont indiqués (voir abréviations à l'annexe 1) que lorsque cela est jugé nécessaire.*

*Pour les* dimensions, *on a suivi le système métrique en n'utilisant comme unités que le mètre (m) et le millimètre (mm). On trouvera à l'annexe 2 des équivalents dans le système anglo-américain. Afin d'éviter la surcharge des plans, il n'a pas toujours été possible d'indiquer les unités. On peut toutefois toujours les reconnaître d'après le contexte et le mode de présentation. Le mètre est utilisé pour les plus grandes dimensions, telles que la longueur des ralingues inférieures, cordes de dos, ralingues des flotteurs, bras, et s'applique aux chiffres composés de nombres entiers suivis de deux décimales (par exemple 5,25; 90,20). Le millimètre est utilisé pour les dimensions plus petites telles que la longueur de la maille (étirée), le diamètre des ralingues, des flotteurs ou des diabolos, ainsi que dans les plans détaillés. Les dimensions en millimètres sont généralement données en nombres entiers seulement (par exemple, 12; 527; 2305), ou avec une décimale seulement (par exemple, 1.2).*

*L'unité de* masse et de poids *est le kilogramme (kg). Des forces telles que la charge de rupture des fils ou des ralingues et la flottabilité des flotteurs, sont données en kilogramme-force (kgf) ou en gramme-force (gf), unités qui, du fait de leur relation avec le kg ou le g, sont jugées plus commodes pour le lecteur que le Newton (N) adopté par le Système international d'unités (1 kgf=9,8 N). On trouvera également à l'annexe 2 les équivalents dans le système anglo-américain.*

*Les* matériaux *sont indiqués par des abréviations fondées de préférence sur des appellations d'usage international courant, telles que plastique (PL), sisal (SIS), polyamide (PA). On en trouvera la liste à l'annexe 1. Un tableau assez complet des noms commerciaux des matériaux synthétiques utilisés dans les engins de pêche, classés en fonction de leurs principaux groupes chimiques, figure à l'annexe 3.*

*La* grosseur des fils *est exprimée conformément au système tex et l'on a adopté le R-Tex comme seule unité car elle est d'application générale. Ce système exprime la "densité linéaire résultante" du fil, c'est-à-dire le poids en grammes de 1 000 m de fil. Pout le monofilament, on donne également*

armamento del arte completo, que sólo tienen por objeto facilitar el estudio, así como los dibujos de detalles de piezas. En lugar de ello se dan las dimensiones esenciales. Sólo se indican los materiales (abreviaturas, Apéndice 1) cuando se considera necesario.

Todas las *dimensiones* son en metros (m) y milímetros (mm). En el Apéndice 2 se dan los equivalentes en el sistema anglo-americano. Para evitar el exceso de datos en los planos, no siempre se pueden indicar las unidades, pero se reconocen por el contexto y la manera de presentarlas. El metro se emplea para las dimensiones mayores, como longitudes de relingas de plomos y flotadores, y se expresa por un número entero seguido de dos decimales (por ejemplo: 5,25; 90,20). El milímetro se emplea para las dimensiones más pequeñas, como claro de malla (estirada), diámetro de cabos, flotadores o bobinas y en los dibujos detallados. Se reconoce porque no hay puntos entre los números (por ejemplo: 12; 527; 2305), o hay un decimal solamente (por ejemplo: 1, 2).

La *masa y el peso* se expresan en kilogramos (kg). Fuerzas tales como la carga de ruptura de los hilos o cabos de redes y la flotabilidad de los flotadores se expresan en kilogramos de fuerza (kgf) o gramos de fuerza (gf) que, por su relación con el kg o el g se consideran más convenientes que la unidad "newton" (N) adoptada por el Sistema Internacional de Unidades (1 kgf=9,8 N). En el Apéndice 2 también se indican los equivalentes en el sistema anglo-americano.

Los *materiales* se expresan por abreviaturas que, de ser posible, se basan en términos de uso internacional común, como plástico (PL), sisal (SIS), poliamido (PA). Aparecen en el Apéndice 1. En el Apéndice 3 se da una tabla bastante completa de los nombres comerciales de los materiales sintéticos empleados en el equipo de pesca, por grupos químicos principales.

Las *dimensiones de los hilos para redes* se expresan en el sistema tex y el R-tex se emplea como unidad única por ser de aplicación general. Indica la "densidad lineal resultante" del hilo para redes terminado, y se obtiene multiplicando su peso en gramos por mil metros. En el caso de los monofilamentos, se indica el diámetro en milímetros, lo que también sirve para distinguirlos de los hilos trenzados o colchados. En los Apéndices 2 y 4 se dan las fórmulas y los cuadros para convertir algunos de los sistemas tradicionales.

La selección de una clase determinada o manera de fabricar el hilo para redes

traditional systems are contained in Appendices 2 and 4.

The selection of a particular type of construction of netting yarn is usually based on the best judgement of the designer with regard to operability and catching efficiency. It may, however, also depend on other considerations, such as availability, price, local preference. The construction given by the designer is therefore not necessarily binding. Consequently, it is indicated only in a few exceptional cases. Recommendations for substitution would be outside the scope of this Catalogue and are therefore left to the judgement of the reader. Some guidance is given by the tables of breaking loads for netting yarns of different materials and constructions in Appendix 4, which include both values, dry unknotted as normally given by the suppliers, and wet knotted which is of greater significance for practical fishing.

In *netting* the type of knot or connexion is specified only when considered essential. The same applies to the orientation of the meshes which is defined as "normal" (N) when it is perpendicular to the general course of the netting yarn in knotted netting, or when it follows the longest possible mesh axis in knotless netting. The relevant symbols are given in Appendix 1.

The *meshsize* is given in millimetres (mm) and defined according to what is commonly called "meshsize stretched", i.e., the distance between the centres of the two opposite knots (or connexions) in the same mesh when fully stretched in the "normal" (N) direction. This corresponds exactly with the practical method of meshsize measurement, i.e., the length of one mesh lumen plus the length of one knot (or connexion). It may be stressed that this is not the same as the "mesh opening" which features in many fisheries regulations. If not otherwise indicated figures followed by mm (millimetre) in the drawings refer to meshsize.

The dimensions of *net panels or sections* in width and length or depth are defined by the number of meshes in a straight row along the edges where applicable. When both edges in one general direction are tapered (e.g., trawl wings, corners) the dimension in this direction is still given along a straight row of meshes even if this actually does not exist. The figures for the number of meshes are arranged in the drawings in such a way that misinterpretation with

le diamètre en millimètres. Cela permet d'indiquer en même temps qu'il s'agit de monofilaments par comparaison avec les fils retors ou tressés. On trouvera aux annexes 2 et 4 des formules et des tables de conversion dans certains systèmes traditionnels.

Le choix d'un type de constitution donné d'un fil de filet repose d'ordinaire sur le meilleur jugement du dessinateur en ce qui concerne sa commodité d'emploi et son efficacité de capture. Il peut toutefois dépendre également d'autres considérations, telles que disponibilité, prix, préférences locales. On n'est donc pas nécessairement tenu de suivre la constitution indiquée par le dessinateur. Par conséquent, elle n'est signalée que dans un petit nombre de cas exceptionnels. Des recommandations préconisant le remplacement de certains types par d'autres sortiraient du cadre du présent catalogue et la question est donc laissée à l'appréciation du lecteur. Des données sur les charges de rupture des fils en différents matériaux et de diverses constitutions figurent dans les tableaux de l'annexe 4 où sont indiquées les deux valeurs: non noué sec, normalement fournie par les fabricants, et noué mouillé, particulièrement importante pour les utilisateurs.

En ce qui concerne l'alèze, le type de noeud ou de liaison n'est spécifié que s'il est important. Il en est de même de l'orientation des mailles qui est qualifiée de "normale" (N) lorsqu'elle perpendiculaire à la direction générale du fil dans les filets noués, ou lorsqu'elle suit l'axe le plus long des mailles dans les filets sans noeuds. Les symboles correspondants sont indiqués à l'annexe 1.

La dimension des mailles *est donnée en millimètres (mm) et correspond à ce que l'on appelle couramment la "longueur de la maille étirée", c'est-à-dire la distance entre les centres des deux noeuds (ou liaisons) se faisant face dans la même maille quand la maille est complètement étirée dans le sens "normal" (N). Cela correspond exactement à la méthode pratique de mesure du maillage, c'est-à-dire la longueur de l'ouverture de la maille plus un noeud (ou liaison). Il convient de souligner que cette mesure est différente de "l'ouverture de maille" qui figure dans de nombreux règlements de pêche. Sauf indication contraire, les chiffres portés en millimètres (mm) dans les plans se rapportent à la dimension des mailles.

Les dimensions des pièces ou sections du filet, *en largeur et en longueur ou profondeur, sont représentées par le nombre de mailles rangées en ligne droite de long des bordures, le cas échéant. Lorsque les

depende de lo que juzgue el proyectista en cuanto a facilidad de manipulación y rendimiento de pesca, aunque también puede depender de consideraciones como disponibilidad, precio, preferencia en el lugar. Por tanto, los datos que da el proyectista no hay que seguirlos al pie de la letra y sólo se dan en unos pocos casos excepcionales. No corresponde a este Catálogo hacer recomendaciones en cuanto a sustitución de materiales, por lo que se deja a la decisión del lector. Se hacen algunas indicaciones en los cuadros de cargas de rotura, de hilos para redes, de materiales de fabricación distintas en el Apéndice 4. Se dan los datos para hilos secos sin anudar como los indican los fabricantes y húmedos anudados que tienen mucha más importancia para la pesca.

En el caso de los *paños de red* la clase de nudo o conexión sólo se indica cuando se considera esencial. Ocurre lo mismo en cuanto a la orientación de las mallas, que se definen como "normal" (N) cuando son perpendiculares a la dirección general del hilo en paños anudados o cuando corresponden a la dirección del mayor eje posible de la malla en paños sin nudos. Los símbolos correspondientes se indican en el Apéndice 1.

Las *dimensiones de la malla* se indican en milímetros (mm) y se definen según lo que se denomina comúnmente "dimensión de la malla estirada", es decir: la distancia entre los centros de los nudos opuestos (o conexiones) de la misma malla totalmente estirada en la dirección "normal" (N), lo que corresponde exactamente al método práctico de medir las mallas, es decir: la longitud de la luz de malla, más la longitud de un nudo (o conexión). Se ha de precisar que esto no es igual que la "abertura de la malla" que figura en muchos reglamentos de pesca. Si no se indica lo contrario, las cifras seguidas de mm (milímetro) en los dibujos se refieren a la dimensión de la malla.

Las dimensiones de los *paños o secciones de red* en anchura y longitud o altura se definen por el número de mallas en una corrida derecha a lo largo de los bordes, cuando esto es posible. Cuando ambos bordes van disminuyendo en una dirección (por ejemplo: bandas, ángulos de una red de arrastre) la dimensión en esta dirección se sigue indicando a lo largo de una corrida derecha de mallas aunque ésta no exista en realidad. Las cifras correspondientes al número de mallas se disponen en los gráficos de manera que se eviten los errores de interpretación en cuanto a la dirección a que se refieren y que se confundan las dimensiones en milímetros (mm). En los

regard to the direction they refer to and confusion with dimensions in millimetres (mm) are excluded. In trawlnet drawings the width of the bosom is given in brackets in addition to the mesh number for the total width of the netting section. When applicable (e.g., for trawls) upper, lower and side panels are denoted by symbols (Appendix 1) to facilitate understanding of the design drawing.

Double-braided netting is mostly restricted to narrow strips along edges or to corners. In such cases the number attached to the symbol for double braiding (Appendix 1) indicates the depth or width in number of meshes which is already included in the number specifying the overall dimension of the respective net panel or section to which the strip or corner of double-braided netting belongs. When whole sections, such as trawl codends, are double-braided, the symbol is attached to the mesh number designating one of the main dimensions of this section, e.g., the length.

For practical reasons the *shape of netting sections* is indicated by the cutting rate at its edges, irrespective of whether hand-braided or shape-cut. Horizontal or vertical edges in the drawing obviously designate straight lines of knots without any bar cuts. For tapered edges point cuts, i.e., cuts of a mesh in "normal" direction are specified by N and full mesh cuts rectangular to "normal" direction by T (transversal). Bar cuts are specified by symbol B; AB indicates all bar cut. In cases where the taper does not follow a reasonably simple cutting rate the next best is given together with a symbol (Appendix 1) indicating its only approximate applicability. A tabulation of common cutting rates for a practical range of taper ratios is given in Appendix 5.

*The hanging ratio* (E), i.e., the length relation between the rope and the netting to be attached to it is defined as the numerical value of the decimal fraction of the length of the rope divided by the stretched length of the respective netting section, the latter being the product of the mesh-size stretched multiplied by the number of meshes in a straight row (e.g. $E = 440$ m/628 m $= 0.70$). It is shown where considered essential, e.g., in purse seines and gillnets, as for instance $E = 0.75$. In all other cases the hanging ratio can be determined if desired by the reader using the above procedure. Changes in the hanging ratio over shorter distances such as in the bosom corners of trawls cannot be shown in the

*deux bordures sont diminuées dans une direction générale (par exemple, ailes de chalut, angles), on continue à indiquer la dimension se rapportant à cette direction suivant une rangée directe de mailles, même si celle-ci n'existe pas dans la réalité. Les chiffres indiqués pour le nombre de mailles sont placés sur les plans de manière à éviter toute erreur d'interprétation concernant la direction à laquelle ils se rapportent et à exclure toute confusion concernant les dimensions en millimètres (mm). Dans les plans de chaluts, la largeur du carré est indiquée entre parenthèses, en sus du nombre de mailles pour la largeur totale de la section du filet. Lorsqu'il y a lieu (par exemple, pour les chaluts), les pièces supérieures, inférieures et latérales sont représentées par des symboles (voir annexe 1) pour faciliter la compréhension des plans.*

*Le laçage double est généralement limité aux bandes étroites que longent les bordures ou aux angles. Dans ces cas, le nombre adjoint aux symboles pour le double laçable (voir annexe 1) indique la profondeur ou la largeur en nombre de mailles qui est déjà inclus dans le nombre spécifiant la dimension globale de la pièce ou section de filet à laquelle appartient la bande ou l'angle d'alèze en double laçage. Lorsque des section entières, telles que les culs de chaluts, sont fabriqués en double laçage, le symbole est joint au nombre de mailles désignant l'une des principales dimensions de cette section, par exemple, la longueur.*

*Pour des raisons pratiques, la forme des pièces d'alèze est indiquée par le processus de coupe à ses bords, qu'ils soient lacés à la main ou taillés en forme. Les bordures horizontales ou verticales sur les plans désignent évidemment des lignes droites de noeuds, sans coupes de pattes. Dans le cas des bordures diminuées, les coupes en maille de côté, c'est-à-dire les coupes d'une maille selon une direction "normale", sont indiquées par la lettre N et les coupes de mailles franches perpendiculaires à la direction "normale" sont indiquées par la lettre T (transversale). Les coupes de pattes sont représentées par la lettre B; AB indique une coupe toutes pattes. Si la diminution ne suit pas un processus de coupe raisonnablement simple, la solution la plus proche donnant les meilleurs résultats est représentée par un symbole (voir annexe 1) indiquant qu'elle n'est applicable que de manière approximative. Un tableau donnant les processus de coupes courants pour une gamme pratique de diminutions figure à l'annexe 5.*

*Le taux d'armement (E), c'est-à-dire le rapport de longueur entre la ralingue et l'alèze qui doit y être jointe, est défini*

planos de redes de arrastre, la anchura del burlón se indica entre paréntesis, además del número de mallas de la anchura total del paño. De ser aplicable (por ejemplo, en el caso de los artes de arrastre), los paños superiores, inferiores y laterales se denotan mediante símbolos (Apéndice 1) para facilitar la interpretación del dibujo.

En general, los paños de hilos trenzados dobles sólo se emplean en franjas estrechas a lo largo de los bordes o en los ángulos. En tales casos el número que figura junto al símbolo que denota el trenzado doble (Apéndice 1) indica la profundidad o anchura del número de mallas que se incluye que da la dimensión total del paño o sección correspondiente al que pertenece la franja o ángulo de paño de hilo trenzado doble. Cuando en secciones enteras, como los sacos de los artes de arrastre, se emplean paños de hilos trenzados dobles, el símbolo se coloca junto al número de mallas que designa una de las principales dimensiones de esta sección, por ejemplo: la longitud.

Por razones prácticas, la *forma de los paños de red* se indica por el tipo de corte en sus bordes, independientemente de que se trencen a mano o se corten según una forma. Los bordes horizontales o verticales de los dibujos designan líneas rectas de nudos sin cortes entre ellos. Los puntos de corte de los bordes en disminución, es decir: los cortes de una malla en dirección "normal", se designan con una N y los cortes de las mallas enteras que forman ángulo recto con la dirección "normal" por una T (transversal). Los cortes entre mallas se designan por el símbolo B; AB indica que se ha cortado todo el entrenudo. En los casos en que los tipos de corte no se pueden hacer de manera sencilla, se presenta la mejor solución junto con un símbolo (Apéndice 1) que indica que su aplicabilidad es sólo aproximada. En el Apéndice 5 figura un cuadro de los tipos de corte comunes para obtener distintas relaciones de disminución.

El *coeficiente de armadura* (E), es decir: la relación entre la longitud de la relinga y la del paño de red que va a soportar es la fracción decimal de la longitud de la relinga dividida por la del paño de red estirado, siendo este último el producto de la dimensión de la malla estirada multiplicado por el número de mallas en una corrida derecha (por ejemplo: $E = 440$ m/628 m $= 0.70$). Sólo se indica cuando se considera esencial, como en el caso de las redes de cerco de jareta y las redes de enmalle (por ejemplo $E = 0,75$). En todos los demás casos el coeficiente de armadura lo puede determinar el lector que lo desee empleando el procedimiento citado. En los

drawing and the interpretation of such rather common features is being left to the judgement of the reader.

*Ropes* are drawn by thick lines and specified by their length in metres, the material and their diameter in millimetres (e.g., 37.20 PES Ø 12). Abbreviations for materials used in rope-making, e.g., for steel wire rope and combination rope are given in Appendix 1, in addition to abbreviations for the natural and synthetic fibre materials used for netting yarns that have been mentioned above. The construction of ropes is not specified. Instead, tables with examples of the comparative properties of some ropes of different materials and construction are given in Appendix 7, which can serve as guidance for selection and eventual substitution.

Because of the variety of items for the specification of *accessories* a certain amount of improvisation had to be accepted. They are mostly shown in the additional detail or schematic drawings and in such a way as to be self-explanatory. Designations by terms or symbols are restricted to the absolute minimum and only the most essential dimensions or properties are given.

As a general rule the vernacular or commercial names have been used to designate the different fish species. Where some doubt still exists, particularly for accurate identification of fish species by their scientific names, reference should be made to the Multilingual Dictionary of Fish and Fish Products (prepared by OECD), the reference work consulted in the preparation of this Catalogue.

The sketches of boats especially showing the deck layout and arrangement of auxiliary equipment for gear handling are given for information purposes only or to facilitate the understanding of the fishing method. Incidentally it is considered advisable to point out that a later work to be published in another series will give details pertaining more directly to boat building.

Whenever for any given type of gear there are two or more variants in construction or manner of use, local adaptations for instance, this is indicated in the title and opposite the drawings by Roman numerals (I, II, etc.). Where these variants refer to only one component part of the gear (for instance the hook or the lure), other possible ways of making this part are shown with the abbreviation ALT (meaning ALTernative).

*comme la valeur numérique d'une fraction dont le numérateur est la longueur de la ralingue et le dénominateur, la longueur étirée de la pièce de filet sur laquelle elle est montée, cette dernière étant elle-même le produit des mailles étirées par le nombre de mailles disposées en rangée droite (par exemple, E=440 m/628 m=0,70). Ce rapport est indiqué lorsqu'il est jugé essentiel, par exemple, dans le cas des sennes coulissantes et des filets maillants (exemple, E=0,75). Dans tous les autres cas, le lecteur peut, s'il le souhaite, calculer le taux d'armement en suivant la méthode indiquée ci-dessus. Les modifications de ce taux sur de petites distances, comme dans les coins des carrés de ventre des chaluts, ne peuvent être indiquées sur les plans et l'interprétation de ces données assez courantes est laissée au lecteur.*

*Les* ralingues *sont représentées par des traits gras avec indication de leur longueur en mètres, de leur matériau et de leur diamètre en millimètres (par exemple, 37,20 PES Ø 12). Les abréviations adoptées pour les ralingues, par exemple pour le filin d'acier et pour le filin mixte, figurent à l'annexe ainsi que les abréviations qui désignent les produits naturels synthétiques utilisés pour les fils, dont il est question plus haut. La constitution des ralingues n'est pas spécifiée, mais des tableaux donnant des exemples des propriétés comparées de certaines ralingues de matériau et de constitution différents figurent à l'annexe 7 et peuvent servir de guides lors du choix ou remplacement de filins.*

*Etant donné la variété des articles pour la spécification des* accessoires, *on a dû accepter une certaine marge d'improvisation. Les accessoires sont surtout indiqués dans les plans de détail ou schématiques conçus pour rendre superflues des explications. Les désignations par appellations ou symboles sont limitées au strict minimum et seules les dimensions ou propriétés essentielles sont données.*

*Pour désigner les différentes espèces de poissons, on a employé d'une manière générale les noms vernaculaires ou commerciaux. Si quelque doute subsiste, en particulier pour l'identification plus précise des espèces par leurs noms scientifiques, il est possible de se reporter au Dictionnaire Multilingue des Poissons et Produits de la Pêche (préparé par l'OCDE), ouvrage de référence consulté pour la préparation du catalogue.*

*Les schémas des bateaux, montrant notamment l'arrangement du pont de pêche et la disposition des auxiliaires servant à la manoeuvre de l'engin, ne sont donnés qu'à*

dibujos no se pueden indicar los cambios en el coeficiente de armadura en secciones cortas como los ángulos del burlón de los artes de arrastre, por lo que la interpretación de estas características se deja al lector.

Los *cabos* están representados por líneas gruesas y se designa su longitud en metros, el material y su diámetro en milímetros (por ejemplo: 37,20 PES Ø 12). Las abreviaturas de los materiales utilizados en elaboración de cabos, entre ellos los relativos al cabo de acero y a la malleta figuran en el Apéndice 1, además de las abreviaturas de los materiales de fibras naturales y sintéticas, ya mencionados, para hilos de redes y cabos. No se indica cómo se han hecho los cabos y en vez de esto, en el Apéndice 7 hay cuadros con ejemplos de las propiedades relativas de algunos cabos de distintos materiales de construcción, que pueden servir como orientación para seleccionar o posiblemente sustituir.

Por ser tantos y tan diversos los *accesorios* se tiene que aceptar una cierta improvisación. Casi todos ellos se reproducen en los detalles adicionales o en esquemas, de manera que no necesiten explicación. La designación por palabras o símbolos se limita al mínimo absoluto y tan sólo se dan las dimensiones o propiedades esenciales.

Para designar las diversas especies de peces se han utilizado, en general, los nombres vulgares o comerciales. Si hubiera alguna duda, sobre todo a propósito de la identificación exacta de las especies por sus nombres científicos, aconsejamos consultar el "Multilingual Dictionary of Fish and Fish Products" (preparado por la OCDE), que ha sido la obra de referencia consultada para la preparación de este Catálogo.

Los esquemas de las embarcaciones, en los que aparece el punto de pesca y la colocación del equipo auxiliar para la maniobra de los artes y aparejos, no se incluyen más que como indicación o para facilitar la comprensión del método de pesca. En otra obra, que se publicará en una serie distinta, se tratará detalladamente de los problemas vinculados más directamente con la construcción naval.

Cuando de un arte o aparejo determinado existen dos o más variantes de construcción o de empleo, debidas, por ejemplo, a adaptaciones locales, las variantes en cuestión se indican en el título y en los diseños con números romanos (por ejemplo, I, II). Si las variantes se refieren solamente a una parte del arte o aparejo (por ejemplo, al anzuelo o al cebo), las diversas posibilidades

As a rule manoeuvres during fishing are shown by sketches representing the main operation stages for shooting or hauling the gear. The sequence of these stages is indicated in Arabic numerals (1, 2, 3 for instance) in order to make a distinction between the different variants of construction or utilization.

Should any complementary information be required on a given gear description, they would be obtained by asking the author mentioned in reference.

*titre indicatif ou pour faciliter la compréhension de la méthode de pêche. A cet égard, nous croyons utile de signaler qu'un ouvrage ultérieur, publié dans une autre série, traitera en détail de ces problèmes plus directement liés à la construction navale.*

*Lorsque pour un type d'engin donné il existe deux ou plusieurs variantes de construction ou d'utilisation correspondant, par exemple, à des adaptations locales, celles-ci sont indiquées dans le titre et en regard des dessins par des chiffres romains (par exemple, I, II). Dans le cas où les variantes ne concernent qu'une partie constitutive de l'engin (par exemple, l'hameçon ou le leurre), les autres possibilités de réalisation de cette partie sont représentées en regard de l'abréviation ALT (pour ALTernative).*

*Les manoeuvres en pêche sont montrées en général par des schémas représentant les principales phases des opérations de mise à l'eau ou de relevage de l'engin. La séquence de ces diverses phases est précisée au moyen de chiffres arabes (par exemple, 1, 2, 3), afin de les distinguer des variantes de construction ou d'utilisation.*

*Dans le cas où une information complémentaire s'avérerait nécessaire pour une description d'engin, elle pourra être obtenue en s'adressant à l'auteur mentionné en référence.*

se indican con la abreviatura ALT (ALTernativa).

Las maniobras de pesca se representan en general con esquemas en los que aparecen las principales fases de las faenas de calado y halado de los artes o aparejos. La secuencia de las diversas fases se indica con números árabes (por ejemplo, 1, 2, 3), para distinguirlas de las variantes de construcción o empleo.

Si es necesaria información adicional para la descripción de un arte, se podrá obtener dirigiéndose al autor mencionado en la referencia.

# III Appendices
## *Annexes*
## Apéndices

# APPENDIX 1

**Abbreviations and symbols used for the designs**
*Abréviations et symboles utilisés pour les plans*
Abreviaciones y símbolos usados en los planos

| | English | *Français* | Español |
|---|---|---|---|
| Alu | = aluminium | *aluminium* | aluminio |
| ALT | = alternative | *alternative* | alternativa |
| BAIT | = bait | *appât* | carnada, cebo |
| BAM | = bamboo | *bambou* | bambú |
| BR | = brass | *cuivre jaune, laiton* | cobre amarillo, latón |
| CEM | = cement | *ciment* | cemento |
| CHRO | = chromium-plated | *chromé* | cromado |
| CK | = cork | *liège* | corcho |
| CLAY | = baked clay | *terre cuite* | tierra cocida |
| COC | = coco | *coco* | coco |
| COMB | = combination rope | *filin mixte* | cabo mixto |
| COT | = cotton | *coton* | algodón |
| COV | = covered, keckled | *garni* | cubierto, aforrado |
| COVER | = cover | *doublage* | camisa |
| CRIN | = horsehair | *crin* | crin |
| Cu | = copper | *cuivre* | cobre |
| CUT | = cut | *coupe* | corte |
| DKN | = double knot | *double noeud* | nudo doble |
| ELEC | = electric | *électrique* | eléctrico |
| FAC | = facultative | *facultatif* | facultativo |
| Fe | = iron | *fer* | hierro |
| FEAT | = feather | *plume* | pluma |
| FISH | = fish | *poisson* | pez |
| GALV | = galvanised | *galvanisé* | galvanizado |
| GL | = glass | *verre* | vidrio |
| HO | = horn | *corne* | cuerno |
| L | = length | *longueur* | longitud |
| LIVE | = live-bait | *appât vivant, vif* | carnada viva |
| MAIS | = maize | *maïs* | maíz |
| MAN | = manila | *manille* | manila |
| MAT | = material | *matériau* | material |
| MET | = metal | *métal* | metal |
| MONO | = monofilament | *monofilament* | monofilamento |
| MOT | = motor | *moteur* | motor |

| | English | Français | Español |
|---|---|---|---|
| NTS | = net sounder | *sondeur de filet* | sonda de la red |
| OS | = bone | *os* | hueso |
| PA | = polyamide | *polyamide* | poliamido |
| Pb | = lead | *plomb* | plomo |
| PE | = polyethylene | *polyéthylène* | polietileno |
| PES | = polyester | *polyester* | poliéster |
| PL | = plastic | *plastique* | plástico |
| PLY | = plywood | *contreplaqué* | madera contraplacada |
| PP | = polypropylene | *polypropylène* | polipropileno |
| PRL | = mother of pearl | *nacre* | madreperla |
| PVA | = polyvinyl alcohol | *alcool de polyvinyle* | alcohol de polivinilo |
| PVC | = polyvinyl chloride | *chlorure de polyvinyle* | cloruro de polivinilo |
| RED | = red | *rouge* | rojo |
| RUB | = rubber | *caoutchouc* | caucho, goma |
| SF | = staple fibre | *schappe* | fibra cortada |
| SH | = shell | *coquille* | concha |
| SIS | = sisal | *sisal* | sisal |
| SQU | = squid | *encornet* | calamar |
| SST | = stainless steel | *acier inoxydable* | acero inoxidable |
| ST | = steel | *acier* | acero |
| SW | = swivel | *émerillon* | grillete giratorio |
| SYN | = synthetic fibre | *fibre synthétique* | fibra sintética |
| TIN | = tinned | *étamé* | hojalata |
| WD | = wood | *bois* | madera |
| WH, WHI | = white | *blanc* | blanco |
| WIRE | = steel wire rope | *câble d'acier* | cable de acero |
| YEL | = yellow | *jaune* | amarillo |
| Zn | = zinc | *zinc* | zinc |

| | English | Français | Español |
|---|---|---|---|
| Ø = | diameter | diamètre | diámetro |
| = | upper panel | dos (face supérieure) | panel superior |
| = | lower panel | ventre (face inférieure) | panel inferior |
| = | side panel | face latérale | panel lateral |
| = | purse ring | anneau de coulisse | anilla |
| = | N-direction in netting | direction N dans le filet | dirección N en la red |
| = | thickness | épaisseur | espesor |
| = | optional | au choix | facultativo |
| ~ = | approximately | approximativement | aproximadamente |
| = | circumference | circonférence | circunferencia |
| = | double braided | lacé double | doble malla |
| = | mesh | maille | malla |
| = | knotless (raschel type) | sans nœuds (type raschel) | sin nudos (tipos raschel) |
| = | knotless (moji type) | sans nœuds (type moji) | sin nudos (tipo moji) |
| = | knotless (twisted type) | sans nœuds (type câblé) | sin nudos (tipo torcido) |
| = | braided | tressé | trenzado |
| = | twisted | câblé | torcido |
| = | current | courant | corriente |
| = | wind | vent | viento |
| = | fish | poisson | pez |

# APPENDIX 2

## Equivalents and conversions
### *Equivalents et conversions*
### Equivalentes y conversiones

General—*Généralités*—Generalidades:

1 metre (m) = 1 000 millimetres (mm)
= 39.37 inch (in.)
= 3.28 feet (ft)
= 1.09 yards (yd)
= 0.55 fathoms (fat)

1 ft = 0.30 m
1 yd = 0.91 m
1 fat = 1.83 m
1 in. = 25.40 mm

1 kilogramme (kg) = 1 000 grammes (g)
= 35.3 ounces (oz)
= 2.21 pounds (lb)

1 oz = 28.35 g
1 lb = 0.45 kg

1 kilogramme-force (kgf) = 9.8 newtons (N)

1 hp = 1 ch = 1 c.v. = 75 kg m/s = 550 ft lb/s = 736 watts (W)

Netting yarns—*Fils pour nappes de filets*—Hilos para paños de red:

tex

**= mass (g) of single yarn per 1000 m**
= *masse (g) du fil simple aux 1000 m*
= masa (g) de hilo sencillo por 1 000 m

R tex

**= mass (g) of finished netting yarn per 1000 m**
= *masse (g) du fil pour nappes de filets fini aux 1000 m*
= masa (g) de hilo para paños de red pronto para uso, por 1 000 m

$$\text{tex} = 0.111 \times \text{Td} = \frac{1\,000}{\text{Nm}} = \frac{590.5}{\text{Ne}_C}$$

$$\text{R tex} = \frac{1\,000\,000}{\text{m/kg}} = \frac{496\,055}{\text{yd/lb}}$$

The R tex value of a netting yarn depends not only on the material but also on its construction (twisting, folding, cabling, braiding) and can therefore not be accurately converted into systems which are based on the single yarns (e.g. Td, Nm, Ne ). If the runnage (m/kg or yd/lb) is not known a rough approximation of the R tex value can be obtained by adding 10% to the product of single yarn size in tex times the number of single yarns in the finished netting yarn.

*La valeur exprimée en R tex d'un fil pour nappes de filets dépend non seulement du matériau mais aussi de son mode de fabrication (torsion, retordage, câblage, tressage) et, par conséquent, elle ne peut pas être convertie avec précision dans des systèmes qui sont basés sur les fils simples (par ex. Td, Nm, Ne ). Si la longueur par unité de masse (m/kg ou yd/lb) n'est pas connue, une approximation grossière de la valeur en R tex peut être obtenue en ajoutant 10% au produit du titre en tex du fil simple par le nombre de fils simples dans le fil pour nappes de filets fini.*

El R tex de un hilo para paños de red depende no sólo del material sino también de la forma en que ha sido manufacturado el hilo (colchado, torsión, cableado, trenzado) y, por tanto, no es posible convertirlo exactamente en sistemas basados en los hilos sencillos (por ejemplo Td, Nm, Ne ). Si no se conoce cuál es la longitud por unidad de masa (m/kg o yd/lb), puede obtenerse el R tex aproximado incrementando en un 10 por ciento el producto del tex del hilo sencillo por el número de hilos sencillos que tiene el hilo para paños de red pronto para el uso.

### Example—*Exemple*—Ejemplo

210 denier × 6 × 3 = 23 tex × 6 × 3 = 414 tex
+ 10% of 414 = 41
_____
R 455 tex

Guidance on the meaning of R tex with regard to runnage (in m/kg) and breaking load is given in the tables of Appendix 4.

*Une indication sur la signification du R tex en ce qui concerne le métrage au kg et la résistance à la rupture est fournie par les tableaux de l'Annexe 4.*

En los cuadros del Apéndice 4 puede verse una indicación de la significación del R tex en cuanto a la longitud por unidad de masa (m/kg) y la resistencia a la rotura.

# APPENDIX 3

## Trade names of synthetic fibres
*Noms commerciaux de fibres synthétiques*
Nombres comerciales de fibras sintéticas

| POLYAMIDE | POLYESTER | POLYETHYLENE | POLYPROPYLENE | POLYVINYL CHLORIDE | POLYVINYL ALCOHOL | COPOLYMER FIBRES |
|---|---|---|---|---|---|---|
| (PA) | (PES) | (PE) | (PP) | (PVC) | (PVA) | |
| Amilan | Dacron | Akvaflex | Akvaflex PP | Envilon | Cremona | Clorène |
| Anid | Diolen | Cerfil | Courlene PY | Fibravyl | Kanebian | Dynel |
| Anzalon | Grilen | Corfiplaste | Danaflex | Rhovyl | Kuralon | Kurehalon |
| Caprolan | Grisuten | Courlene | Drylene 6 | | Kuremona | Saran |
| Dederon | Tergal | Drylene 3 | Hostalen PP (HD) | | Manryo | Teviron |
| Enkalon | Terital | Etylon | Meraklon | | Mewlon | Velon |
| Forlion | Terlenka | Hiralon | Multiflex | | Trawlon | Vinitron |
| Kapron | Tetoron | Hi-Zex | Nufil | | Vinalon | Wynene |
| Kenlon | Terylene | Hostalen G | Prolene | | Vinylon | |
| Knoxlock | Trevira | Laveten | Propylon | | | |
| Lilion | | Levilene | Ribofil | | | |
| Nailon | | Marlin PE | Trofil P | | | |
| Nailonsix | | Norfil | Ulstron | | | |
| Nylon | | Northylen | Velon P | | | |
| Perlon | | Nymplex | Vestolen P | | | |
| Platil | | Rigidex | | | | |
| Relon | | Trofil | | | | |
| Roblon | | Velon PS (LP) | | | | |
| Silon | | Vestolen A | | | | |
| Stilon | | | | | | |

---

## Trade names of combination netting yarns
*Noms commerciaux de fils composites pour filet*
Nombres comerciales de hilos compuestos para redes

| | |
|---|---|
| Kyokurin | PA cont. fil. plus Saran |
| Livlon | PA cont. fil. plus Saran |
| Marlon A | PA cont. fil. plus PVA st. |
| Marlon B | PA cont. fil. plus Saran |
| Marlon C | PA cont. fil. plus PVC cont. fil. |
| Marlon D | PA cont. fil. plus Saran |
| Marlon E | PA st. plus PVA (or PVC) st. |
| Marumoron | PA cont. fil. plus PVA st. |
| Polex | PE plus Saran |
| Polysara | PE plus Saran |
| Polytex | PE plus PVC cont. fil. |
| Ryolon | PES cont. fil. plus PVC cont. fil. |
| Saran-N | PA cont. fil. plus Saran |
| Tailon (Tylon-P) | PA cont. fil. plus PA st. |
| Temimew | PVA st. plus PVC st. |

cont. fil. = **continuous filament**—*filament continu*—filamento continuo

st. = **staple fibre**—*schappe*—fibra cortada

# APPENDIX 4

### Examples of common netting yarns
*Exemples de fils courants pour nappes de filets*
Ejemplos de hilos ordinarios para paños de red
(G. Klust, Hamburg)

A=**dry, unknotted**—*sec non noué*—seco, sin nudos:
B=**wet, knotted**—*mouillé noué*—mojado, con nudos:
  **value for one yarn**—*valeur pour un fil*—valor para un hilo

| R tex | m/kg | Breaking load *Résistance à la rupture* Resistencia a la rotura | | R tex | m/kg | Breaking load *Résistance à la rupture* Resistencia a la rotura | |
|---|---|---|---|---|---|---|---|
| | | A kgf | B kgf | | | A kgf | B kgf |

## POLYAMIDE (PA)

**Twisted, filament**—*Câblé, filament*—Trenzado, filamento:

| R tex | m/kg | A kgf | B kgf | R tex | m/kg | A kgf | B kgf |
|---|---|---|---|---|---|---|---|
| 50 | 20000 | 3.1 | 1.8 | 1250 | 800 | 58 | 32 |
| 75 | 13300 | 4.6 | 2.7 | 1300 | 770 | 63 | 35 |
| 100 | 10000 | 6.2 | 3.6 | 1500 | 670 | 67 | 37 |
| 155 | 6460 | 8 | 5 | 1600 | 625 | 76 | 43 |
| 240 | 4170 | 14 | 9 | 2000 | 500 | 99 | 52 |
| 320 | 3130 | 18 | 11 | 2600 | 385 | 138 | 73 |
| 400 | 2500 | 21 | 13 | 3180 | 315 | 157 | 80 |
| 480 | 2080 | 25 | 15 | 3400 | 294 | 178 | 85 |
| 550 | 1820 | 30 | 18 | 4000 | 250 | 210 | 100 |
| 650 | 1540 | 34 | 20 | 5000 | 200 | 260 | 125 |
| 720 | 1390 | 40 | 22 | 5700 | 175 | 330 | 150 |
| 800 | 1250 | 42 | 24 | 6800 | 147 | 360 | 165 |
| 900 | 1100 | 47 | 26 | 8350 | 120 | 440 | 200 |
| 1000 | 1000 | 49 | 27 | 11200 | 90 | 560 | 250 |
| 1100 | 900 | 50 | 28 | | | | |

**Braided, filament**—*Tressé, filament*—Colchado, filamento:

| R tex | m/kg | A kgf | B kgf | R tex | m/kg | A kgf | B kgf |
|---|---|---|---|---|---|---|---|
| 1350 | 740 | 82 | 44 | 4900 | 205 | 255 | 125 |
| 1550 | 645 | 92 | 48 | 7000 | 140 | 346 | 170 |
| 1700 | 590 | 95 | 51 | 8800 | 114 | 418 | 205 |
| 1960 | 510 | 102 | 60 | 9600 | 104 | 460 | 220 |
| 2460 | 400 | 130 | 73 | 10600 | 94 | 515 | 245 |
| 2820 | 350 | 146 | 81 | 12200 | 82 | 590 | 280 |
| 3500 | 290 | 172 | 85 | 13800 | 72 | 650 | 310 |
| 4300 | 230 | 224 | 110 | 17500 | 57 | 800 | 360 |

## POLYPROPYLENE (PP)

**Twisted, filament**—*Câblé, filament*—Trenzado, filamento:

| R tex | m/kg | A kgf | B kgf | R tex | m/kg | A kgf | B kgf |
|---|---|---|---|---|---|---|---|
| 210 | 4760 | 13 | 8 | 1440 | 690 | 71 | 36 |
| 290 | 3470 | 15 | 9 | 1920 | 520 | 92 | 47 |
| 360 | 2780 | 19 | 11 | 2290 | 440 | 112 | 59 |
| 430 | 2330 | 25 | 14 | 2820 | 350 | 132 | 70 |
| 550 | 1820 | 28 | 15 | 3300 | 300 | 152 | 80 |
| 640 | 1560 | 38 | 19 | 4700 | 210 | 190 | 100 |
| 920 | 1090 | 44 | 23 | 5640 | 177 | 254 | 130 |
| 1190 | 840 | 58 | 30 | | | | |

| R tex | m/kg | Breaking load *Résistance à la rupture* Resistencia a la rotura | | R tex | m/kg | Breaking load *Résistance à la rupture* Resistencia a la rotura | |
|---|---|---|---|---|---|---|---|
| | | A kgf | B kgf | | | A kgf | B kgf |

**Twisted, split fibre**—*Câblé, fibrillé*—Colchada, fibras cortas:

| R tex | m/kg | A kgf | B kgf | R tex | m/kg | A kgf | B kgf |
|---|---|---|---|---|---|---|---|
| 210 | 4760 | 9 | 6 | 2360 | 420 | 86 | 54 |
| 300 | 3330 | 13 | 9 | 307C | 325 | 100 | 59 |
| 390 | 2560 | 18 | 12 | 4100 | 240 | 150 | 88 |
| 800 | 1250 | 32 | 22 | 5400 | 185 | 215 | 120 |
| 990 | 1010 | 38 | 24 | 6660 | 150 | 300 | 170 |
| 1390 | 720 | 57 | 36 | | | | |
| 1900 | 530 | 73 | 46 | | | | |

# POLYETHYLENE (PE)

**Twisted or braided, wire**—*Câblé ou tressé, filament épais*—Colchado o trenzado, filamento espeso:

| R tex | m/kg | A kgf | B kgf | R tex | m/kg | A kgf | B kgf |
|---|---|---|---|---|---|---|---|
| 190 | 5260 | 7.5 | 5.5 | 2800 | 360 | 93 | 67 |
| 370 | 2700 | 10 | 7 | 3400 | 294 | 116 | 83 |
| 700 | 1430 | 27 | 19 | 4440 | 225 | 135 | 97 |
| 1050 | 950 | 36 | 24 | 5300 | 190 | 170 | 125 |
| 1410 | 710 | 49 | 35 | 7680 | 130 | 218 | 160 |
| 1760 | 570 | 60 | 84 | 10100 | 100 | 290 | 210 |
| 2170 | 460 | 75 | 54 | | | | |

# POLYAMIDE (PA)

**Monofilament**—*monofilament*—monofilamento:

| Ø mm | A kgf | B kgf | Ø mm | A kgf | B kgf |
|---|---|---|---|---|---|
| 0.10 | 0.5 | 0.2 | 1.10 | 45 | 25 |
| 0.15 | 1.5 | 0.6 | 1.20 | 50 | 28 |
| 0.20 | 2.3 | 1.2 | 1.30 | 65 | 35 |
| 0.25 | 3.8 | 1.9 | 1.40 | 73 | 40 |
| 0.30 | 4.9 | 2.7 | 1.50 | 85 | 47 |
| 0.35 | 6.3 | 3.2 | 1.60 | 100 | 52 |
| 0.40 | 7.6 | 4.3 | 1.70 | 110 | 58 |
| 0.45 | 11.5 | 5.5 | 1.80 | 120 | 63 |
| 0.50 | 12.7 | 6.5 | 1.90 | 130 | 72 |
| 0.55 | 14 | 7.5 | 2.00 | 145 | 75 |
| 0.60 | 17 | 8.5 | 2.50 | 220 | 112 |
| 0.70 | 24 | 12.5 | | | |
| 0.80 | 29 | 15 | | | |
| 0.90 | 36 | 19 | | | |
| 1.00 | 42 | 22 | | | |

# APPENDIX 5

### Cutting rates and taper ratio
*Processus de coupe et taux de diminution*
Tipos de cortes y relación de disminuciones

The shape of the pieces of netting of which a gear consists is achieved by increasing or reducing the number of meshes in width or length. This can be done by hand braiding or by shape cutting of which the latter is by far the most common. In this catalogue the shape of net sections is therefore specified in cutting rates only which can be converted into any hand braiding scheme by the reader himself.

The cutting rate gives the rhythmical combination of different types of cuts, either along a row of sequential knots (N or T cuts, see figures 1 and 2) or parallel to a line of sequential mesh bars (B cuts, see figure 3).

It is indicated for the N and T cuts by the number of consecutive meshes cut and for the B cuts by the number of consecutive bars severed along the cutting edge, not counting the bars on the preceding point (knot).

The following combinations are used for cutting netting to shape:

N and B cuts (example 1N2B, figure 4)

T and B cuts (example 1T2B, figure 5)

N and T cuts (example 1N2T, figure 6)

AB or all bar cuts (figure 3)

The taper ratio indicates the relation between the number of meshes lost (or gained) counted in the T direction at the end of the depth of the cut which is counted in meshes in the N direction.

In order to facilitate repairs, modifications or designs of nets, the following table gives the most common cutting rates in correspondence with the respective taper ratios.

*La forme des pièces de filet dont un engin est constitué s'obtient par accroissement ou réduction du nombre des mailles en hauteur ou en largeur. On peut y parvenir par laçage manuel ou par coupe, ce dernier procédé étant de loin le plus courant. Dans ce catalogue, on a donc indiqué la forme des pièces de filet uniquement par les processus de coupe que le lecteur pourra lui-même convertir en termes de laçage manuel.*

*Le processus de coupe donne la combinaison rythmique des divers types de coupe, soit en suivant un rang de noeuds consécutifs (coupe N ou T, voir Figures 1 et 2), soit parallèlement à une ligne de pattes consécutives (coupe B, voir Figure 3).*

*Il est indiqué pour les coupes N et T par le nombre de mailles consécutives coupées, et pour les coupes B par le nombre de pattes consécutives sectionnées selon la bordure de découpage, sans compter les pattes du noeud de maille de côté précédent.*

*Ou utilise les combinaisons suivantes pour couper le filet:*

*Coupes N et B (exemple 1N2B, figure 4)*

*Coupes T et B (exemple 1T2B, figure 5)*

*Coupes N et T (exemple 1N2T, figure 6)*

*Coupes AB ou toutes pattes (figure 3)*

*Le taux de diminution indique le rapport entre le nombre de mailles perdues (ou gagnées) comptées dans là direction T à la fin de la profondur de la coupe qui est comptée en mailles dans la direction N.*

*Afin de faciliter le ramendage, la modification ou le dessin des filets, le tableau ci-joint donne les coupes les plus courantes avec les taux de diminution correspondants.*

Se da forma a los paños de redes que constituyen el arte, aumentando o disminuyendo el número de mallas en longitud o anchura y esto se hace trenzando a mano o cortando el paño, procedimiento este último que es con mucho el más empleado, razón por la cual en este catálogo la forma de las secciones de las redes sólo se expresará en tipos de cortes, que el lector puede convertir en cualquiera de los diversos trenzados a mano.

Los tipos de cortes dan una combinación rítmica de todas ellas, bien a lo largo de una corrida de nudos consecutivos (cortes N o T, véanse las figuras 1 y 2) o paralelos a una línea de entrenudos consecutivos (cortes B, véase figura 3). En el caso de N y T, se indica por el número de mallas consecutivas cortadas y en el de los cortes B por el número de entrenudos consecutivos cortados a lo largo del borde de corte, sin contar los entrenudos del nudo de malla lateral anterior.

Para dar forma a los paños se emplean las combinaciones siguientes:

Cortes N y B (ejemplo 1N2B, figura 4)

Cortes T y B (ejemplo 1T2B, figura 5)

Cortes N y T (ejemplo 1N2T, figura 6)

AB o todos los cortes de entrenudos (figura 3)

La proporción de reducción indica la relación entre el número de mallas disminuido (o aumentado) contado en la dirección T en la parte más distante del corte, que se cuenta en mallas en la dirección N.

Para facilitar las reparaciones, hacer modificaciones o cambiar las formas de las redes, en la tabla siguiente se indican los tipos de cortes más comunes que corresponden a las disminuciones respectivas.

# Common Cutting Rates and Taper Ratios
*Processus courants de coupe et diminutions*
Tipos corrientes de corte y relación de disminuciones

**Number of meshes lost (or gained)**
*Nombre de mailles tombées (ou augmentées)*
Número de mallas disminuidas (o aumentadas)

**Number of meshes in depth** / *Nombre de mailles de chute* / Número de mallas de altura

|    | 1 | 2 | 3 | 4 | 5 | 6 | 7 | 8 | 9 | 10 |
|----|-----|-----|------|------|------|------|------|------|------|------|
| 1  | AB | 1T2B | 1T1B | 3T2B | 2T1B | 5T2B | 3T1B | 7T2B | 4T1B | 9T2B |
| 2  | 1N2B | AB | 1T4B | 1T2B | 3T4B | 1T1B | 5T4B | 3T2B | 7T4B | 2T1B |
| 3  | 1N1B | 1N4B | AB | 1T6B | 1T3B | 1T2B | 2T3B | 6T6B | 1T1B | 7T6B |
| 4  | 3N2B | 1N2B | 1N6B | AB | 1T8B | 1T4B | 3T8B | 1T2B | 5T8B | 3T4B |
| 5  | 2N1B | 3N4B | 1N3B | 1N8B | AB | 1T10B | 1T5B | 3T10B | 2T5B | 1T2B |
| 6  | 5N2B | 1N1B | 1N2B | 1N4B | 1N10B | AB | 1T12B | 1T6B | 1T4B | 1T3B |
| 7  | 3N1B | 5N4B | 2N3B | 3N8B | 1N5B | 1N12B | AB | 1T14B | 1T7B | 3T14B |
| 8  | 7N2B | 3N2B | 5N6B | 1N2B | 3N10B | 1N6B | 1N14B | AB | 1T16B | 1T8B |
| 9  | 4N1B | 7N4B | 1N1B | 5N8B | 2N5B | 1N4B | 1N7B | 1N16B | AB | 1T18B |
| 10 | 9N2B | 2N1B | 7N6B | 3N4B | 1N2B | 1N3B | 3N14B | 1N8B | 1N18B | AB |
| 11 | 5N1B | 9N4B | 4N3B | 7N8B | 3N5B | 5N12B | 2N7B | 3N16B | 1N9B | 1N20B |
| 12 | 11N2B | 5N2B | 3N2B | 1N1B | 7N10B | 1N2B | 5N14B | 1N4B | 1N6B | 1N10B |
| 13 | 6N1B | 11N4B | 5N3B | 9N8B | 4N5B | 7N12B | 3N7B | 5N16B | 2N9B | 3N20B |
| 14 | 13N2B | 3N1B | 11N6B | 5N4B | 9N10B | 2N3B | 1N2B | 3N8B | 5N18B | 1N5B |
| 15 | 7N1B | 13N4B | 2N1B | 11N8B | 1N1B | 3N4B | 4N7B | 7N16B | 1N3B | 1N4B |
| 16 | 15N2B | 7N2B | 13N6B | 3N2B | 11N10B | 5N6B | 9N14B | 1N2B | 7N18B | 3N10B |
| 17 | 8N1B | 15N4B | 7N3B | 13N8B | 6N5B | 11N12B | 5N7B | 9N16B | 4N9B | 7N20B |
| 18 | 17N2B | 4N1B | 5N2B | 7N4B | 13N10B | 1N1B | 11N14B | 5N8B | 1N2B | 2N5B |
| 19 | 9N1B | 17N4B | 8N3B | 15N8B | 7N5B | 13N12B | 6N7B | 11N16B | 5N9B | 9N20B |

course of yarn
direction du fil
dirección del hilo

**Figure 1. N cut ("normal"). The cut is perpendicular to the general course of the yarn in knotted netting.**

*Figure 1. Coupe N ("normale"). La coupe est perpendiculaire à la direction générale du fil dans du filet noué.*

Figura 1. Corte N ("normal"). El corte es perpendicular a la dirección general del hilo en la red anudada.

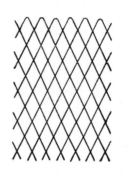

direction of cut
direction de coupe
dirección del corte

course of yarn
direction du fil
dirección del hilo

**Figure 2. T cut ("transversal"). The cut is parallel to the general direction of the yarn in knotted netting.**

*Figure 2. Coupe T ("transversale"). La coupe est parallèle à la direction générale du fil dans du filet noué.*

Figura 2. Corte T ("transversal"). El corte es paralelo a la dirección general del hilo en la red anudada.

direction of cut
direction de coupe
dirección del corte

**Figure 3. B cut ("bar"). The cut is parallel to a line of sequential mesh bars.**

*Figure 3. Coupe B ("biaise"). La coupe est parallèle à une série rectiligne de côtés de mailles.*

Figura 3. Corte B ("bies"). El corte es paralelo a una serie rectilínea de los lados de las mallas.

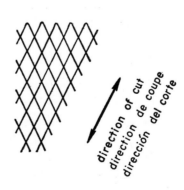

direction of cut
direction de coupe
dirección del corte

24

**Figure 4. Cutting rate 1N2B.**

*Figure 4. Processus de coupe 1N2B.*

Figura 4. Proceso de corte 1N2B

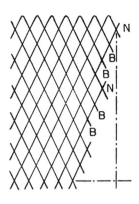

**Figure 5. Cutting rate 1T2B.**

*Figure 5. Processus de coupe 1T2B.*

Figura 5. Proceso de corte 1T2B.

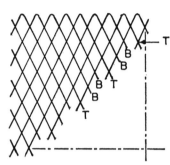

**Figure 6. Cutting rate 1N2T.**

*Figure 6. Processus de coupe 1N2T.*

Figura 6. Proceso de corte 1N2T.

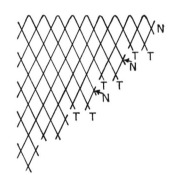

# APPENDIX 6

### Hanging ratio
*Taux d'armement*
Coeficiente de armadura

The term hanging ratio (symbol E) designates the ratio between the length of a given portion of mounting rope and the length of the stretched netting hung on this portion of rope (figure 7).

The hanging ratio may be written as a decimal fraction, or as a vulgar fraction, or as a percentage, such as in the following example:

E=0.50 or E=1/2 or E=50%

In this catalogue, the decimal fraction has been specified only. It is, however, of interest to point out that the corresponding vulgar fraction can be used in common practice for net mounting. For instance, with E=0.50 or 1/2, we have two meshes mounted on the length of one stretched mesh. Also, following the same method, with E=0.80 or 4/5, we have five meshes mounted on the length of four stretched meshes. More generally speaking, when the hanging ratio can be expressed by a vulgar fraction, the denominator of this fraction represents the number of mounted meshes and the numerator the number of meshes, the stretched length of which corresponds to that of the rope.

*Le terme taux d'armement (symbole E) désigne le rapport entre la longueur d'une portion donnée de ralingue et la longueur du filet étiré monté sur cette portion de ralingue (figure 7).*

*Le taux d'armement peut être indiqué par une fraction décimale, ou par une fraction ordinaire, ou par un pourcentage, comme dans l'exemple suivant:*

*E=0.50 ou E=1/2 ou E=50%*

*Dans ce catalogue, on a indiqué seulement la fraction décimale. Il est cependant intéressant de noter que la fraction ordinaire correspondante peut être utilisée dans la pratique courante du montage des filets. C'est ainsi que pour E=0.50 ou 1/2, on a 2 mailles montées sur la longueur de 1 maille étirée. Aussi, suivant la même méthode, pour E=0.80 ou 4/5, on a 5 mailles montées sur la longueur de 4 mailles étirées. D'une manière générale, quand le taux d'armement peut être exprimé par une fraction ordinaire, le dénominateur de cette fraction représente le nombre des mailles montées et le numérateur le nombre de mailles dont la longueur étirée correspond à celle de la ralingue.*

El término "coeficiente de armamento" (símbolo E) se refiere a la relación que existe entre la longitud de una porción dada de relinga y la longitud de la red estirada montada sobre esta porción de relinga (figura 7).

El coeficiente de armamento puede ser indicado por una fracción decimal, por una fracción ordinaria o por un porcentaje, como en el ejemplo siguiente:

E=0.50 ó E=1/2 ó E=50%.

En este catálogo se ha indicado solamente la fracción decimal. Sin embargo, es interesante señalar que la fracción ordinaria correspondiente puede ser utilizada en la práctica corriente para armar las redes. Por ejemplo, E=0.50 ó 1/2, tenemos 2 mallas montadas sobre la longitud de 1 malla estirada. Asimismo, siguiendo el mismo método, E=0.80 ó 4/5, tenemos 5 mallas montadas sobre la longitud de 4 mallas estiradas. En general, cuando el coeficiente de armamento puede ser expresado por una fracción ordinaria, el denominador de esta fracción representa el número de mallas montadas y el numerador, el número de mallas cuya longitud estirada corresponde a la de la relinga.

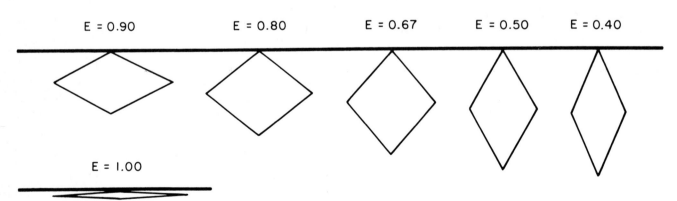

**Figure 7. Usual hanging ratios (E).**

*Figure 7. Taux d'armement courants (E).*

Figura 7. Coeficientes usuales de armadura (E).

# APPENDIX 7

**Examples of synthetic fibre ropes, hawser lay**
*Exemples de cordages en fibre synthétique, commettage d'aussière*
Ejemplos de cabo de fibra sintética, colchado para calabrotes
(G. Klust, Hamburg)

C = **mass/length**—*masse/longueur*—masa/longitud:

D = **breaking load**—*résistance à la rupture*—resistencia a la rotura:

| Ø | Polyamide (PA) | | Polyester (PES) | | Polypropylene (PP) | | Polyethylene (PE) | |
|---|---|---|---|---|---|---|---|---|
| | C | D | C | D | C | D | C | D |
| mm | kg/100m | kgf | kg/100m | kgf | kg/100m | kgf | kg/100m | kgf |
| 4 | 1.1 | 320 | 1.4 | 295 | — | — | — | — |
| 6 | 2.4 | 750 | 3 | 565 | 1.7 | 550 | 1.7 | 400 |
| 8 | 4.2 | 1,350 | 5.1 | 1,020 | 3 | 960 | 3 | 685 |
| 10 | 6.5 | 2,080 | 8.1 | 1,590 | 4.5 | 1,425 | 4.7 | 1,010 |
| 12 | 9.4 | 3,000 | 11.6 | 2,270 | 6.5 | 2,030 | 6.7 | 1,450 |
| 14 | 12.8 | 4,100 | 15.7 | 3,180 | 9 | 2,790 | 9.1 | 1,950 |
| 16 | 16.6 | 5,300 | 20.5 | 4,060 | 11.5 | 3,500 | 12 | 2,520 |
| 18 | 21 | 6,700 | 26 | 5,080 | 14.8 | 4,450 | 15 | 3,020 |
| 20 | 26 | 8,300 | 32 | 6,350 | 18 | 5,370 | 18.6 | 3,720 |
| 22 | 31.5 | 10,000 | 38.4 | 7,620 | 22 | 6,500 | 22.5 | 4,500 |
| 24 | 37.5 | 12,000 | 46 | 9,140 | 26 | 7,600 | 27 | 5,250 |
| 26 | 44 | 14,000 | 53.7 | 10,700 | 30.5 | 8,900 | 31.5 | 6,130 |
| 28 | 51 | 15,800 | 63 | 12,200 | 35.5 | 10,100 | 36.5 | 7,080 |
| 30 | 58.5 | 17,800 | 71.9 | 13,700 | 40.5 | 11,500 | 42 | 8,050 |
| 32 | 66.5 | 20,000 | 82 | 15,700 | 46 | 12,800 | 47.6 | 9,150 |
| 36 | 84 | 24,800 | 104 | 19,300 | 58.5 | 16,100 | 60 | 11,400 |
| 40 | 104 | 30,000 | 128 | 23,900 | 72 | 19,400 | 74.5 | 14,000 |

# APPENDIX 8

**Glossary of fishing gear terms**
*Glossaire de termes d'engins de pêche*
Glosario de términos de aparejos de pesca

| | | |
|---|---|---|
| A. aimed trawling | chalutage contrôlé | arrastre dirigido |
| anchor seining (Danish seining) | pêche à la senne danoise au mouillage | pesca con red de cerco danesa |
| angle of attack (of trawl board) | angle d'attaque (de panneau de chalut) | ángulo de ataque (de puertas de arte de arrastre) |
| B. backstrop | patte (de panneau de chalut) | pata de gallo (de las puertas) |
| bag, bunt | poche, sac | copo del arte |
| bagnet | filet trappe | red de copo |
| bait | appât | cebo |
| baitings | (1) diminutions | (1) reducción de mallas |
| | (2) petit dos | (2) casarete, cazarete |
| ballast | lest | lastre |
| bar (of mesh) | patte (côté de la maille) | pie (lado de la malla) |
| basket (of longline) | panier (de palangre) | cesto (de palangre) |
| beach seine | senne de plage | arte de playa, atarraya |
| beamtrawl | chalut à perche | arte de arrastre de vara, vara de barra |
| becket | erse | estrobo |
| belly (of trawlnet) | ventre (de chalut) | vientre (de arte de arrastre) |
| bellyline | barrette de ventre | barreta |
| boat seine | senne de bateau | red de cerco |
| bobbin (of groundrope) | diabolos, sphères (de bourrelet) | bolas, diábolos, esféricos (de relinga inferior o de plomos) |
| bolchline | filière | trencilla |
| bonding | fixation | fijación |
| bosom (of trawlnet) | carré (de chalut) | bocana (de arte de arrastre) |
| bottom-set | calé sur le fond | calado en el fondo |
| bottom trawl | chalut de fond | arte de arrastre en el fondo |
| bracket (of trawl board) | branchon (de panneau de chalut) | triángulo (de puerta de arte de arrastre) |
| braided (netting yarn) | tressé (fil pour filet) | trenzado (hilo para red) |
| braiding (of netting) | laçage (de filet) | trenzado (de la red) |
| brailer | salabarde | salabardo |
| branchline | avançon | brazolada |
| breaking load | résistance à la rupture | resistencia a la rotura |
| bull trawl | chalut-boeuf | red de pareja |
| bunt (of purse seine) | poche (de senne coulissante) | copo (de arte de cerco de jareta) |
| buoyancy | flottabilité | flotabilidad |
| buoylight | feu ou fanal de bouée | boya luminosa |
| butterfly (of trawl) | guindineau, triangle (de chalut) | calón (de red de arrastre) |
| C. chafer (for codend) | tablier (pour cul de chalut) | parpala (del copo) |
| codend (of trawlnet) | cul (de chalut) | saco, copo (de arte de arrastre) |
| codline (of trawlnet) | raban de cul (de chalut) | sereta (de arte de arrastre) |
| coil (of rope) | glène (de filin) | rollo (de cabo) |
| coir | coco | coco |

| | | |
|---|---|---|
| combination rope | filin mixte | alambrada, cabo mixto |
| crowfoot | patte d'oie | pie de gallo |
| cutting rate (of netting) | processus de coupe (de filet) | tipo de corte (de paños de red) |
| D. Danish seine | senne danoise | red danesa |
| danleno | guindineau | calón |
| depressor | plongeur | depresor |
| dipnet | filet soulevé | salabardo |
| disc roller (for groundrope) | diabolo plat (pour bourrelet) | diábolo, rodillo (de relinga de plomos) |
| double knot | double noeud | nudo doble |
| double rig (trawling) | gréement double (chalutage) | aparejo doble (arrastre) |
| dredge | drague | draga, rastra |
| driftnet | filet dérivant | arte de deriva |
| E. elasticity (of netting yarn) | élasticité (de fil pour filet) | elasticidad (del hilo para red) |
| elongation (of netting yarn) | allongement (de fil pour filet) | alargamiento (del hilo para red) |
| end bracket | gousset d'extrémité | pie de gallo |
| eye splice | oeil épissé | gaza |
| F. fishing lamp | lampe de pêche | lámpara de pesca |
| fish pump | pompe à poisson | bomba para peces |
| flapper (of trawlnet) | voile, tambour (de chalut) | trampa (de la red de arrastre) |
| fleet (of nets) | tésure | andana (de redes) |
| float | flotteur | flotador |
| floatline | ralingue de flotteurs | relinga alta, de corchos |
| fly-dragging (Danish seining) | dragage à la volée (pêche à la senne danoise) | pescar en marcha (con red danesa) |
| flying mesh or flymesh | maille folle | malla libre, angola |
| foam plastic | mousse de plastique | plástico poroso |
| footrope | bourrelet, ralingue inférieure | relinga inferior |
| front weight | poids antérieur | peso anterior |
| full mesh (in cutting of netting) | maille franche (en coupe de filet) | malla franca (en la reducción de la red) |
| funnel | entonnoir | embudo |
| G. gear (for fishing) | engin (pour la pêche) | arte de pesca |
| G-hook | croc en G | gancho en G |
| gillnet | filet maillant | red de enmalle |
| grassrope (of trawl) | bourrelet de coco (de chalut) | relinga de bonote (de arte de arrastre) |
| groundrope | bourrelet | relinga de plomos |
| H. halving back, see splitting strop | | |
| handline | ligne à main | aparejo, línea de mano |
| hanging (of netting) | montage, armement (d'un filet) | armar un arte |
| hanging ratio | taux d'armement | coeficiente de armadura |
| headline | corde de dos | relinga de corchos |
| heaving bag | double poche extérieure | saco de izar |
| high opening trawl | chalut à grande ouverture verticale | arte de arrastre de mucha abertura vertical |
| hook | hameçon | anzuelo |
| hook shaft | tige de l'hameçon, hampe | brazo del anzuelo |
| hook tip | pointe de l'hameçon, ardillon | punta del gancho, muerte |
| hoop | cerceau | cercar, rodear, cerco |
| hydrofoil (trawl board) | hydrodynamique (panneau de chalut) | hidrodinámica (puerta de arte de arrastre) |
| I. inflatable float | flotteur gonflable | flotador |
| J. jig | faux | muestra |
| joining (of net sections) | aboutere, collage (de pièces de filet) | unión (de paños de red) |
| K. kelly's eye | huit | ocho |
| kite | plateau élévateur | elevador |

| | | |
|---|---|---|
| knot | *noeud* | nudo |
| knotless netting, Raschel | *filet sans noeuds, Raschel* | red sin nudos, Raschel |
| knotless netting, twisted | *filet sans noeuds, retordu* | red sin nudos, colchada |
| L. lacing | *transfilage* | pasar una randa, ligadura, atadura |
| lampara net | *filet lamparo* | mamparra |
| lastridge (of trawlnet) | *ralingue de côté (de chalut)* | relinga de costado (de arte de arrastre) |
| lay (of rope, etc.) | *commettage (d'un filin, etc.)* | colchado (de un cabo, etc.) |
| lazyline | *baîllon, hale-à-bord* | vira-vira |
| leadline | *ralingue plombée* | relinga de plomos |
| leg (of trawl) | *patte (de chalut)* | pernada |
| lengthening piece (of trawlnet) | *rallonge (de chalut)* | antecopo, manga (de arte de arrastre) |
| liftnet | *carrelet* | balanza, medio mundo |
| light fishing | *pêche à la lumière* | pesca con luz |
| line | *ligne* | línea |
| links (of chain) | *maillons (de chaîne)* | eslabones (de cadena) |
| live bait | *appât vivant* | cebo vivo |
| longline | *palangre, corde* | palangre |
| longliner | *palangrier, cordier* | buque palangrero |
| lure | *leurre* | añagaza |
| M. mainline (of longline) | *ligne principale (de palangre)* | línea, línea madre |
| mesh | *maille* | malla |
| meshsize (stretched) | *longueur de la maille (étirée)* | longitud de malla (estirada) |
| midwater trawl | *chalut pélagique* | arte de arrastre pelágico |
| monofilament | *monofilament* | monofilamento |
| mudrope (of trawl) | *bourrelet pour fond de vase (de chalut)* | relinga de plomos para fondos sucios |
| multifilament | *multifilament* | multifilamento |
| N. net | *filet* | red |
| netting | *nappe de filet, alèze* | paño de red |
| netting yarn | *fil pour filet* | hilo para redes |
| O. opening type (purse ring) | *anneau de coulisse du type ouvrant* | anillas que se pueden abrir |
| otter board, see trawl board | | |
| otter trawl | *chalut à panneaux* | arte de arrastre de puertas |
| outrigger | *tangon* | tangón, botalón |
| overhand knot | *noeud simple* | nudo llano |
| P. pair trawl | *chalut-boeuf* | arrastre de pareja |
| panel (of net) | *face (de filet)* | paño |
| patent link | *maillon breveté* | eslabón de patente |
| pelagic trawl, see midwater trawl | | |
| pennant | *rapporteur* | falsa boza |
| plaited (netting yarn) | *tressé (fil pour filet)* | trenzado (hilo para redes) |
| point (in cutting of netting) | *maille de côté (en coupe de filet)* | malla de costado (corte de paños) |
| poke, pork line, see lazyline | | |
| pole and line (tuna fishing) | *canne (pêche du thon)* | pesca con caña (pesca de atún) |
| pony board | *poney* | puerta de calón |
| pot | *nasse, casier* | nasa |
| pot warp | *orin de casier* | cabo de nasa |
| pound net | *filet piège* | almadraba, trampa |
| preservation (of yarns, etc.) | *conservation (des fils, etc.)* | conservación |
| pursed lampara net | *filet lampara coulissant* | mampara de cerco |
| purse line | *coulisse* | jareta |
| purse ring | *anneau de coulisse* | anilla |

| | | |
|---|---|---|
| purse ring bridle | *pantoire d'anneau de coulisse* | cabo de anillas, rabiza de anilla |
| purse seine | *senne coulissante, bolinche* | red de cerco de jareta |
| purse seiner | *senneur* | embarcación que pesca al cerco, cerquero |
| Q. quarter point | *triangle d'aile (au-coin de carré)* | triángulo de banda |
| quarter rope | *parpaillot, biribi* | vira-vira, parpallón |
| R. Raschel, see knotless netting | | |
| recessed link | *maille à méplats* | eslabón ranurado |
| reef knot | *noeud plat* | nudo llano |
| rig (of gear) | *gréement (d'engin)* | armazón (del arte) |
| ringnet | *filet tournant* | red de cerco |
| roller (for groundrope) | *diabolo (pour bourrelet)* | diábolo, rodillo (para relinga de plomos) |
| rope | *filin, cordage* | cabo |
| runnage | *longueur par unité de poids* | longitud por unidad de peso |
| S. scoop net | *épuisette, haveneau* | salabardo |
| seam (of net) | *couture (de filet)* | costura (de red) |
| seine | *senne* | red de cerco |
| seiner | *senneur* | cerquero |
| selvedge | *bordure renforcée* | enchace, borde, costura |
| semi-pelagic trawl | *chalut semi-pélagique* | arte de arrastre semipelágico |
| set gillnet | *filet maillant calé* | red de enmalle fija |
| setnet | *filet calé* | red fija |
| shackle | *manille* | grillete |
| shear-chain | *chaîne d'écartement* | cadena de refuerzo |
| sheet bend, or weaver knot | *noeud d'écoute ou de tisserand* | vuelta de escota, nudo de tejedor |
| shoe plate (of trawl board) | *élement de semelle (de panneau de chalut)* | zapata (de puerta de arrastre) |
| shrimp trawl | *chalut à crevette* | arte camaronero |
| shrimp trawler | *crevettier* | camaronero (embarcación) |
| shrinkage (of yarn, etc.) | *retrait au mouillag (de fil, etc.)* | contracción |
| sidestream | *couture latérale* | costura lateral |
| side trawler | *chalutier latéral* | arrastrero por el costado |
| sinker | *lest* | plomo |
| snood | *empile* | tanza |
| spacer disc (for groundrope) | *intermédiare (de bourrelet)* | separador (del burlón) |
| splitting strop | *erse de cul* | estrobo de saco |
| square (of trawlnet) | *grand dos (de chalut)* | cielo, visera |
| stake | *pieu* | estaca, poste, pilote |
| stakenet | *haut-parc et bas-parc* | arte de estacada |
| staple fibre | *fibre discontinue, schappe* | fibra corta |
| sterntrawler | *chalutier arrière* | arrastrero por popa |
| stick-held dipnet | *filet soulevé soutenu par un bâton* | salabardo con mango |
| stow net | *diable, chalut à l'étalage* | biturón |
| strand (of yarns) | *toron (de fil)* | cordón (de hilo) |
| strengthening rope | *filin de renfort, ralingue* | cabo de refuerzo, relinga |
| strip (of netting) | *bande (de filet) ou nappe* | paño (piezas de redes) |
| strop | *erse* | estrobo |
| sunk driftnet | *filet dérivant en profondeur* | red de deriva en profundidad |
| surrounding net | *filet encerclant* | red de cerco |
| sweepline, sweep | *bras* | malleta |
| swivel | *émerillon* | grillete giratorio |
| T. take-up (of meshes) | *recrue (de mailles)* | aumento (de mallas) |
| tanglenet | *folle, filet emmêlant* | red de enmalle |
| tapering | *diminution* | reducción |

| | | |
|---|---|---|
| taper ratio | *rapport de diminution* | índice de reducción |
| throat (of fyke net) | *gorget, tambour (de verveux)* | garganta (biturón con alas) |
| tickler chain | *chaîne gratteuse* | cadena para levantar camarón |
| trammelnet | *trémail* | trasmallo |
| trapnet | *filet piège* | nasa, trampa |
| trawl board | *panneau de chalut* | puerta del arte |
| trawler | *chalutier* | arrastrero |
| trawl gear | *engin de chalutage* | arte de arrastre |
| trawlnet | *chalut* | red de arrastre |
| troller | *bateau de pêche à la traîne* | curricanero |
| trolling | *pêche à la traîne* | pesca a la cacea |
| trynet (for shrimp trawling) | *chalut d'essai (pour chalutage à la crevette)* | red de ensayo (para pescar camarón al arrastre) |
| twine | *fil, fil retors* | hilo |
| twist factor (of yarn) | *coefficient de torsion (de fil)* | coeficiente de torsión (del hilo) |
| V. vinge trawl, see wing trawl | | |
| W. warp (for trawl) | *fune (de chalut)* | cable de arrastre |
| weaver knot (or sheet bend) | *noeud de tisserand (ou noeud d'écoute)* | nudo de tejedor (vuelta de escota) |
| webbing, see netting | | |
| wing (of trawlnet) | *aile (de chalut)* | ala, bandas, pernadas |
| wingtip | *pointe d'aile* | extremo de la banda |
| wing trawl | *chalut à grande ouverture verticale* | red a gran abertura vertical |
| wire rope | *filin d'acier* | cable, cable de acero |
| Y. yarn, see netting yarn | | |
| Z. zipper line | *ligne de transfilage* | matafión, cabos para dividir los cercos de jareta |
| zipper ring | *anneau pour transfilage* | anillas de los cabos de división del gran cerco de jareta |

# IV Designs and specifications
## *Plans et spécifications*
## Planos y especificaciones

34

# SURROUNDING NET
Purse seine
Sardinella
Senegal

# FILET TOURNANT
Senne coulissante
Sardinelle
Senegal

# RED DE CERCO
Red de cerco de jareta
Alacha
Senegal

REFERENCE
G. Grasset
FAO

| VESSEL | BATEAU | BARCO | |
|--------|--------|-------|------|
| Loa | Lht | Et | 14 m |
| GT | TJB | TB | – |
| hp | ch | cv | 15 |

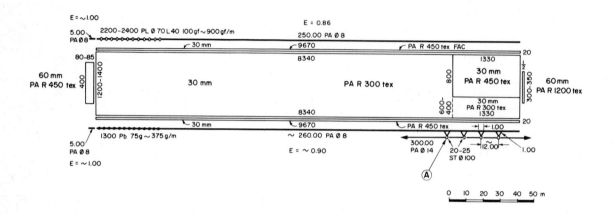

(A)

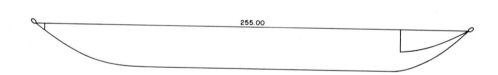

255.00

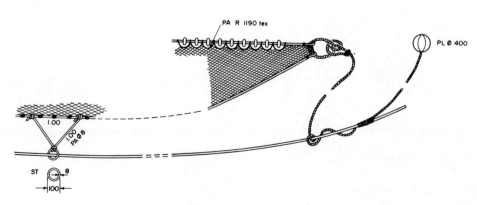

PA R 1190 tex

PL Ø 400

ST 8

1.00

1.00 PA Ø 8

**40**

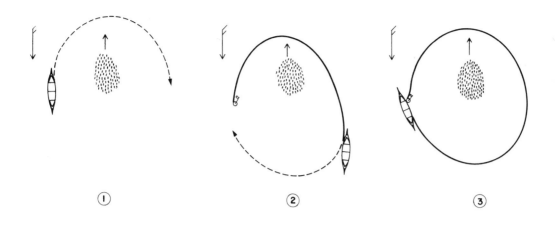

① ② ③

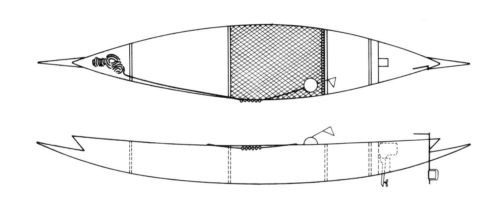

Photos N.J. Scheffers, FAO

## SURROUNDING NET
Purse seine
Sardine
Mediterranean, France
I  Night fishing
II Day fishing

## FILET TOURNANT
Senne coulissante
Sardine
Méditerranée, France
I  Pêche de nuit
II Pêche de jour

## RED DE CERCO
Red de cerco de jareta
Sardina
Mediterráneo, Francia
I  Pesca de noche
II Pesca de día

### REFERENCE
M. Cardone, P.Y. Dremière
Institut des Pêches Maritimes
Sète, France

| VESSEL | BATEAU | BARCO | |
|---|---|---|---|
| Loa | Lht | Et | 13-15 m |
| GT | TJB | TB | - |
| hp | ch | cv | 150-200 |

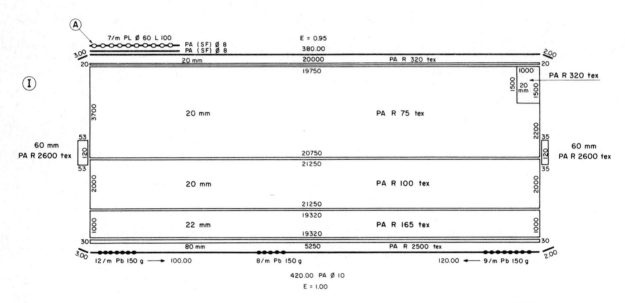

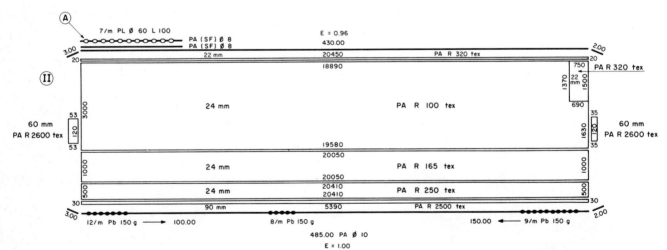

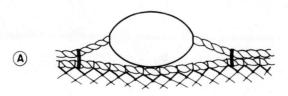

(A)

42

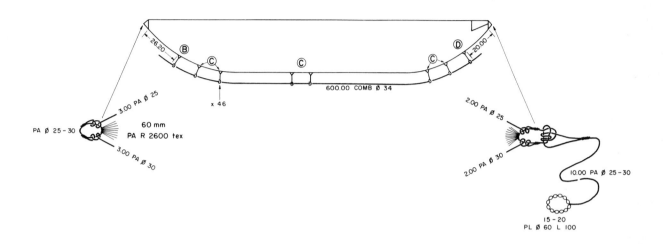

26.20

Ⓑ    Ⓒ         Ⓒ                    Ⓒ    Ⓓ    20.00

3.00 PA Ø 25

PA Ø 25-30

60 mm
PA R 2600 tex

3.00 PA Ø 30

x 46

600.00 COMB Ø 34

2.00 PA Ø 25

2.00 PA Ø 30

10.00 PA Ø 25-30

15 - 20
PL Ø 60 L 100

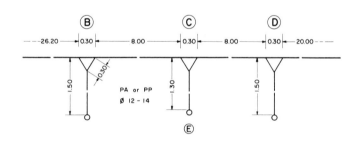

Ⓑ           Ⓒ           Ⓓ

---26.20 ---|--0.30--|---- 8.00 ----|--0.30--|---- 8.00 ----|--0.30--|-- 20.00 ----

1.50     0.30      1.30            1.50

PA or PP
Ø 12-14

Ⓔ

12 Fe

Ⓔ (x 46)

200

# SURROUNDING NET
Purse seine
Acanthobrama terrae-sanctae
Lake Kinereth, Israel

# FILET TOURNANT
Senne coulissante
Acanthobrama terrae-sanctae
Lac Kinereth, Israël

# RED DE CERCO
Red de cerco de jareta
Acanthobrama terrae-sanctae
Lago Kinereth, Israel

### REFERENCE
M. Ben-Yami, E. Grofit
Department of Fisheries
Fisheries Technology Unit
Haifa, Israel

| VESSEL | BATEAU | BARCO | |
|---|---|---|---|
| Loa | Lht | Et | 10-12 m |
| GT | TJB | TB | - |
| hp | ch | cv | - |

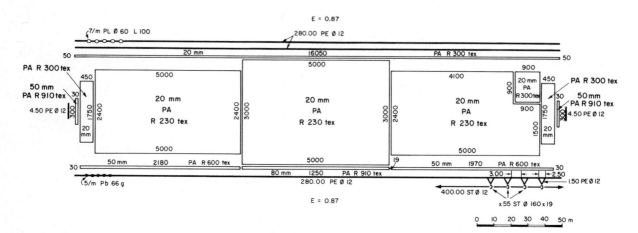

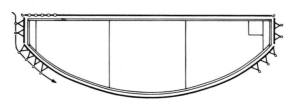

8000 c    x 2-3

44

## SURROUNDING NET
Purse seine
Sardine
California, U.S.A.

## FILET TOURNANT
Senne coulissante
Sardine
Californie, E.U.

## RED DE CERCO
Red de cerco de jareta
Sardina
California, EE.UU.

### REFERENCE
Borti Petrich
U.S. Net and Twine Co.
1596 Judson Avenue
Long Beach, Calif. 90810
U.S.A.

### VESSEL  BATEAU  BARCO

| Loa | Lht | Et | 15 m |
|-----|-----|-----|------|
| GT  | TJB | TB | –    |
| hp  | ch  | cv | 150  |

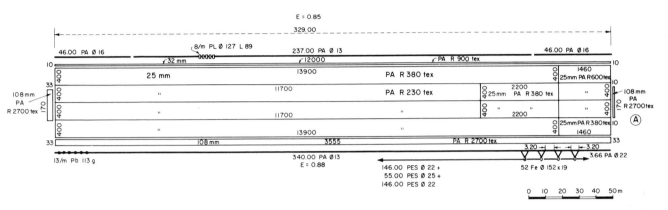

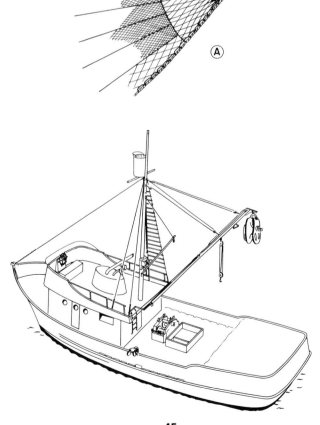

(A)

45

## SURROUNDING NET
Purse seine
Tilapia
Lake Galilee, Israel

## FILET TOURNANT
Senne coulissante
Tilapia
Lac de Galilée, Israël

## RED DE CERCO
Red de cerco de jareta
Tilapia
Lago Galilea, Israel

### REFERENCE
M. Ben Yami, E. Grofit
Department of Fisheries
Fisheries Technology Unit
Haifa, Israel

VESSEL  BATEAU  BARCO

| Loa | Lht | Et | 10-12 m |
|-----|-----|-----|---------|
| GT | TJB | TB | – |
| hp | ch | cv | – |

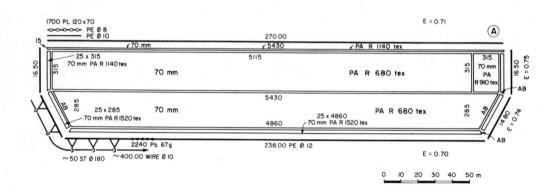

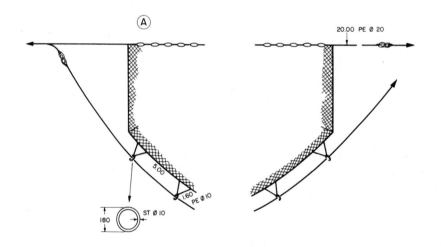

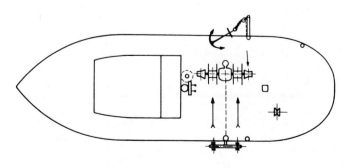

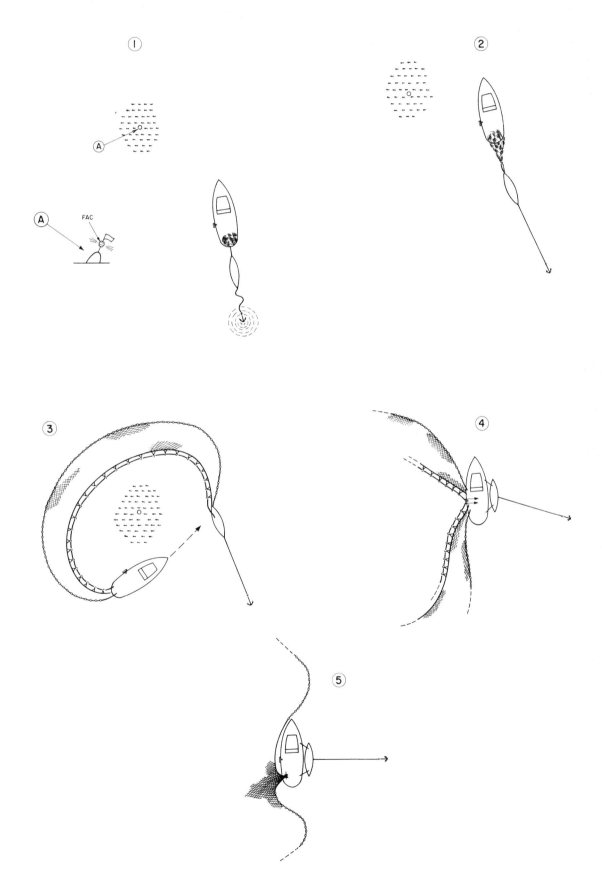

SURROUNDING NET
Ring net, two-boat
Ndagala
Lake Tanganyika, Burundi

FILET TOURNANT
Ring net, à deux bateaux
Ndagala
Lac Tanganika, Burundi

RED DE CERCO
Ring net, con dos barcos
Ndagala
Lago Tanganyika, Burundi

REFERENCE
A. Collart, L. Haling, E. Andrianos
FAO

VESSEL  BATEAU  BARCO

| | | | |
|---|---|---|---|
| Loa | Lht | Et | 15 m + 10 m |
| GT | TJB | TB | – – |
| hp | ch | cv | 120-150 |

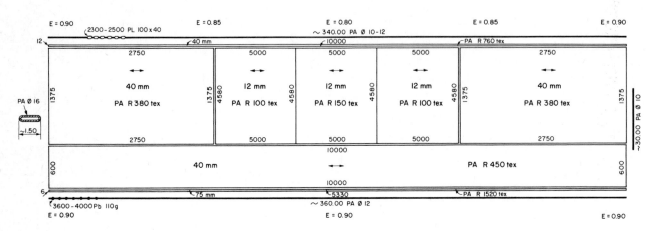

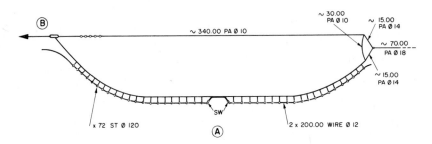

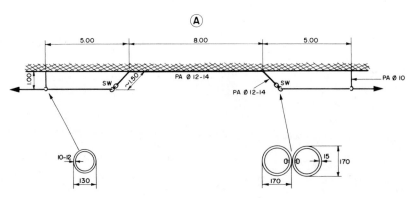

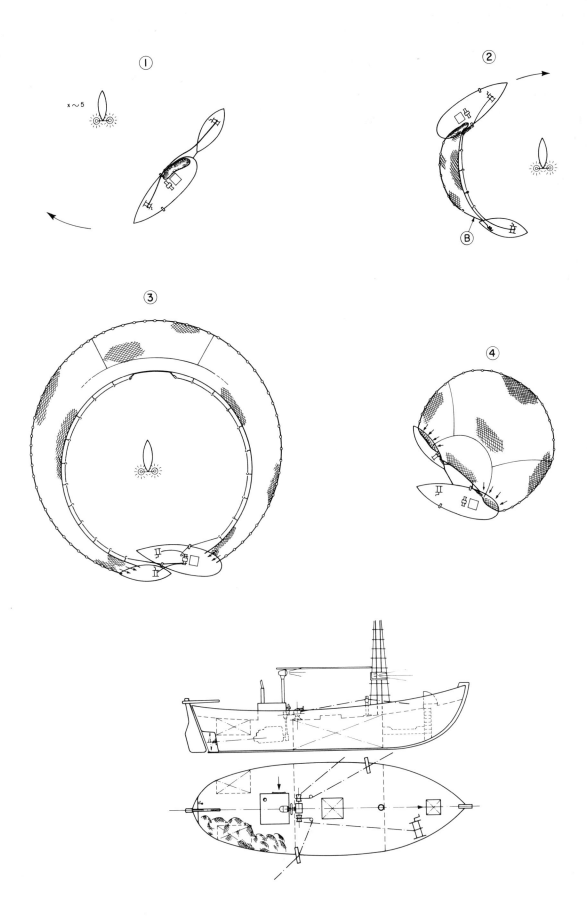

SURROUNDING NET
Chiromila, with purse line
Kapenta (= Dagaa)
Lake Tanganyika, Zambia

FILET TOURNANT
Chiromila, avec coulisse
Kapenta (= Dagaa)
Lac Tanganika, Zambie

RED DE CERCO
Chiromila, con jareta
Kapenta (= Dagaa)
Lago Tanganyika, Zambia

REFERENCE
G.W. Coulter, L. Haling, Y.A. Znamensky
FAO

VESSEL BATEAU BARCO
Loa    Lht    Et    9 m
GT     TJB    TB    –
hp     ch     cv    –

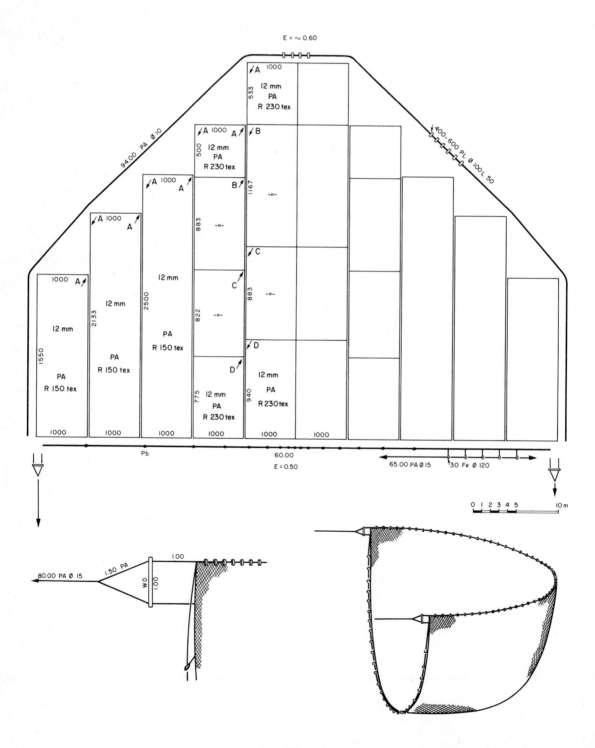

50

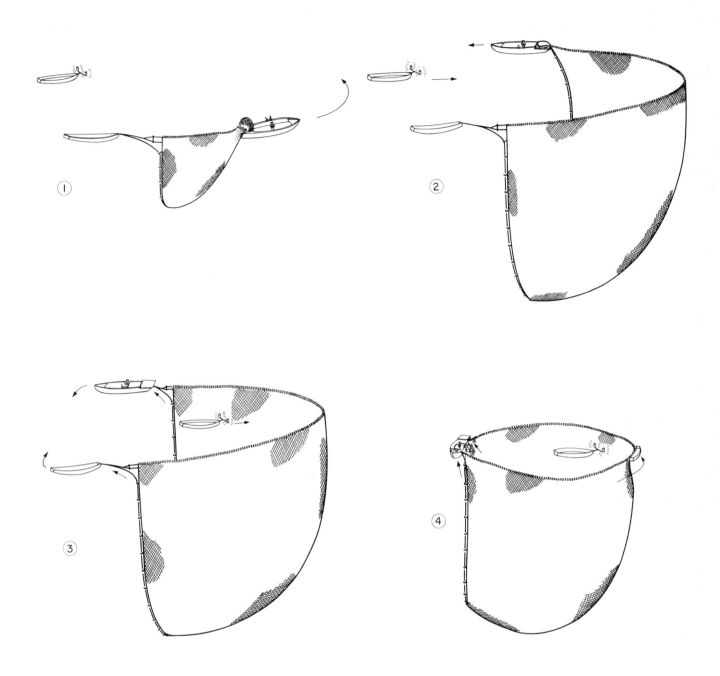

SURROUNDING NET
Lampara
For catching live-bait
California, U.S.A.

FILET TOURNANT
Lampara
Pour pêche d'appât vivant
Californie, E.U.

RED DE CERCO
Lampara
Para pescar la carnada viva
California, EE.UU.

REFERENCE
T.V. Carter
1301 West Eleventh Street
Long Beach, Calif. 90813
U.S.A.

VESSEL BATEAU BARCO
| | | | |
|---|---|---|---|
| Loa | Lht | Et | 8-15 m |
| GT | TJB | TB | – |
| hp | ch | cv | – |

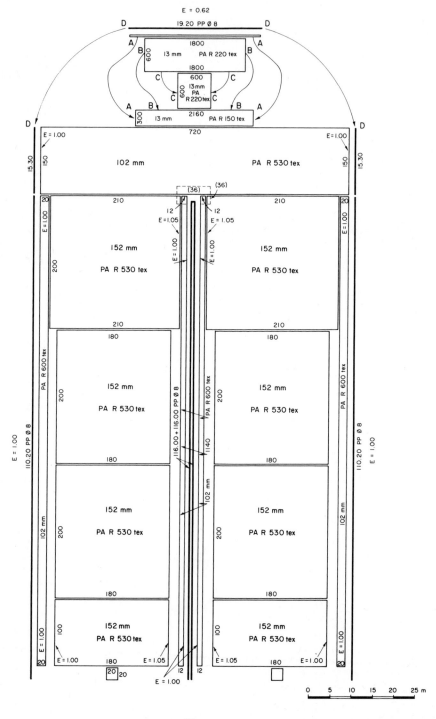

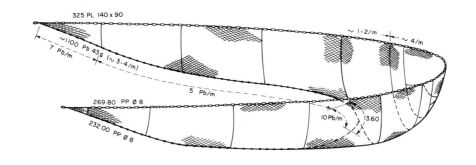

325 PL 140 x 90

~1100 Pb 43g (~3-4/m)
7 Pb/m

~1-2/m     ~4/m

5 Pb/m

269.80 PP Ø 8
232.00 PP Ø 8

10 Pb/m     13.60

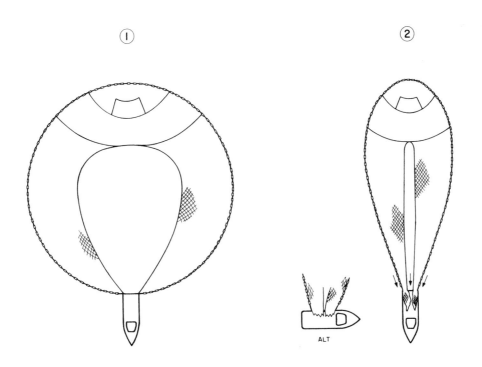

①

②

ALT

## SEINE NET
Beach seine, without bag
Freshwater fishes
Rivers and swamps, Nigeria

## SENNE
Senne de plage, sans poche
Poissons d'eau douce
Rivières et marais, Nigeria

## RED DE TIRO
Arte de playa, sin saco
Peces de agua dulce
Ríos y marismas, Nigeria

REFERENCE
W. Reed

FAO

| VESSEL | BATEAU | BARCO | |
|--------|--------|-------|---|
| Loa | Lht | Et | 4-5 m |
| GT | TJB | TB | - |
| hp | ch | cv | - |

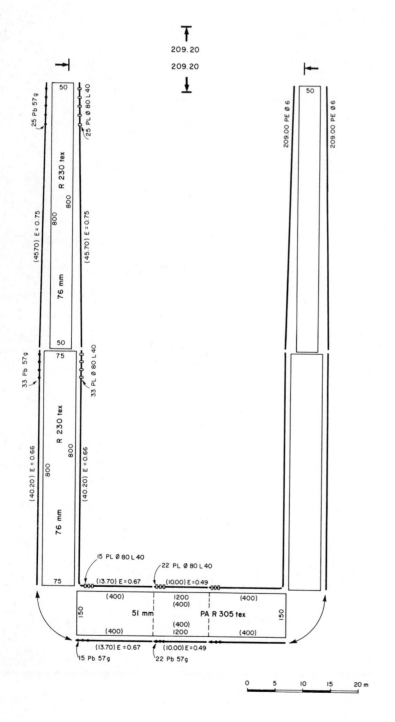

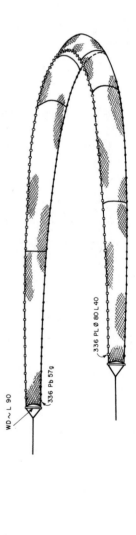

0    5    10    15    20 m

## SEINE NET
Beach seine, without bag
Sandeel
Saint-Pierre and Miquelon
North-West Atlantic

## SENNE
Senne de plage, sans poche
Lançon
Saint-Pierre et Miquelon
Atlantique Nord-Ouest

## RED DE TIRO
Arte de playa, sin saco
Lanzones
Saint Pierre y Miquelón
Atlántico Noroeste

REFERENCE
B. Paturel
Institut des Pêches Maritimes
Saint-Pierre et Miquelon
Amérique du Nord

| VESSEL | BATEAU | BARCO | |
|---|---|---|---|
| Loa | Lht | Et | 8 m |
| GT | TJB | TB | - |
| hp | ch | cv | 15-25 |

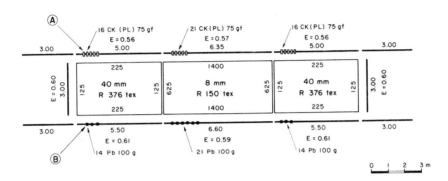

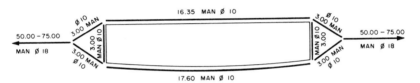

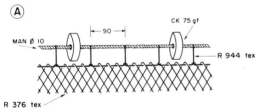

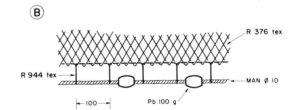

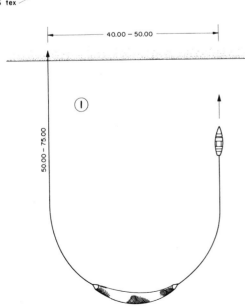

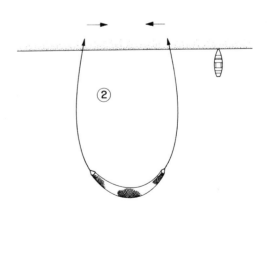

55

# SEINE NET
Beach seine, with bag
Sandeel
Mediterranean, France

# SENNE
Senne de plage, avec poche
Lançon
Méditerranée, France

# RED DE TIRO
Arte de playa, con saco
Lanzones
Mediterráneo, Francia

REFERENCE
M. Catania, P.Y. Dremière
Institut des Pêches Maritimes
Sète, France

VESSEL  BATEAU  BARCO

| | | | |
|---|---|---|---|
| Loa | Lht | Et | 6 m |
| GT | TJB | TB | - |
| hp | ch | cv | 20 |

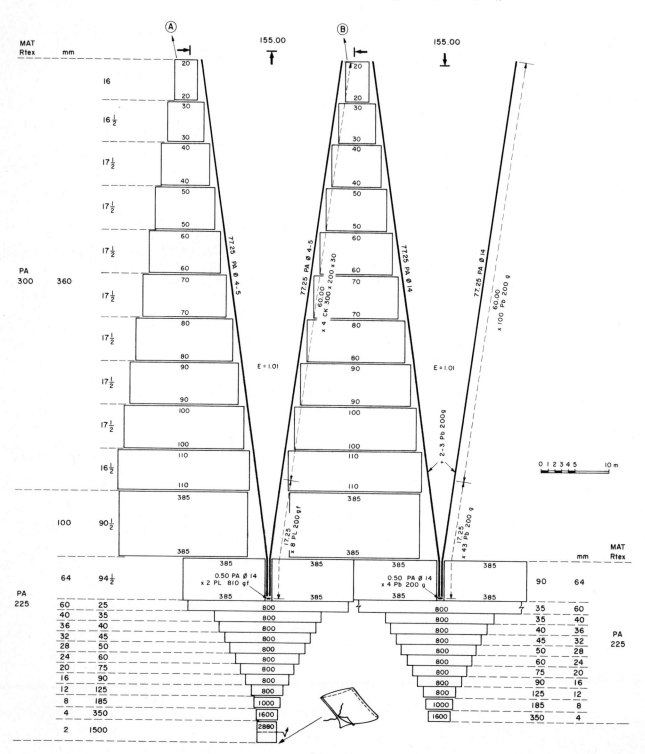

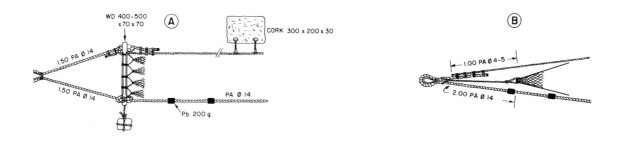

WD 400-500
x70 x70  Ⓐ

1.50 PA Ø 14

1.50 PA Ø 14

CORK 300 x 200 x 30

PA Ø 14

Pb 200 g

Ⓑ

1.00 PA Ø 4-5

2.00 PA Ø 14

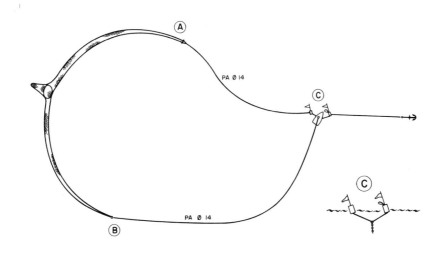

Ⓐ

PA Ø 14

Ⓒ

Ⓑ

PA Ø 14

Ⓒ

## SEINE NET
Beach seine, without bag
Sardinella, pelagic and bottom fishes
Senegal

## SENNE
Senne de plage, sans poche
Sardinelle, poissons pélagiques et démersaux
Sénégal

## RED DE TIRO
Arte de playa, sin saco
Alacha, peces pelágicos y de fondo
Senegal

REFERENCE
P.A. Seck
c/o Direction de l'Océanographie et des Pêches
Dakar, Sénégal

VESSEL  BATEAU  BARCO

| Loa | Lht | Et | 12-14 m |
|-----|-----|-----|---------|
| GT | TJB | TB | - |
| hp | ch | cv | - |

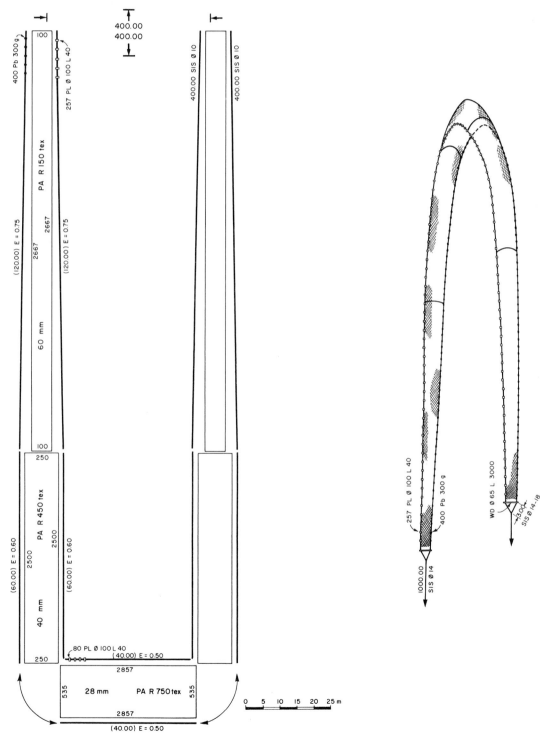

400.00
400.00

400 Pb 300 g

100

257 PL Ø 100 L 40

PA R 150 tex

2667    2667

60 mm

(1200.0) E = 0.75    (120.00) E = 0.75

400.00 SIS Ø 10    400.00 SIS Ø 10

100

250    250

PA R 450 tex

2500    2500

40 mm

(60.00) E = 0.60    (60.00) E = 0.60

250

80 PL Ø 100 L 40
(40.00) E = 0.50

2857

535    28 mm    PA R 750 tex    535

2857

(40.00) E = 0.50

257 PL Ø 100 L 40    400 Pb 300 g

WD Ø 65 L 3000

SIS Ø 14-18

3000

1000.00    SIS Ø 14

0  5  10  15  20  25 m

**59**

## SEINE NET

Boat seine, with bag
Freshwater fishes
Lakes, Northern Germany (Fed. Rep.)
I.  a: boat-operated, with hauling line
    b: shore-operated, with hauling line
II. boat-operated, without hauling line

## SENNE

Senne de bateau, avec poche
Poissons d'eau douce
Lacs, Allemagne du Nord (Rép. Féd.)
I.  a: manoeuvrée du bateau, avec câble de halage
    b: manoeuvrée du rivage, avec câble de halage
II. manoeuvrée du bateau, sans ralingue de halage

## RED DE TIRO

Chinchorro, en barco, con saco
Peces de agua dulce
Lagos, Norte de Alemania (Rep. fed.)
I.  a: maniobrado desde el barco,
        con cable de halado
    b: maniobrado desde la ribera,
        con cable de halado
II. maniobrado desde el barco, sin
        cable de halado

### REFERENCE

M. Kaulin
Maxburgstrasse, 13
6735 Maikammer, Fed. Rep. of Germany

A. v. Brandt
Karlestrasse, 32
2 Hamburg 76, Fed. Rep. of Germany

| VESSEL | BATEAU | BARCO | X 2 |
|--------|--------|-------|-----|
| Loa | Lht | Et | 7-8 m |
| GT | TJB | TB | - |
| hp | .ch | cv | - |

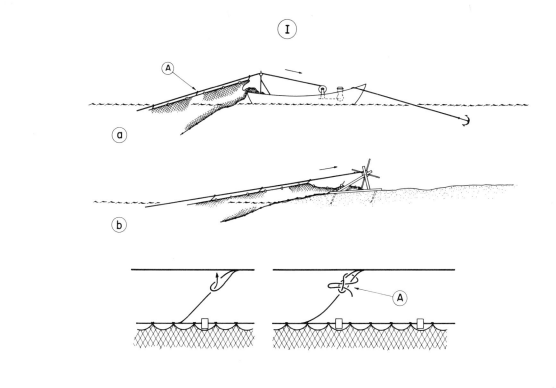

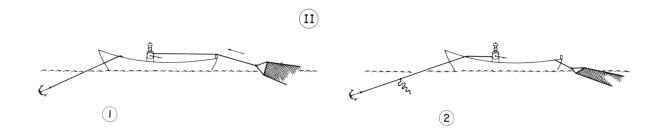

Bottom seine
Haddock, whiting, cod
Scotland
I.  Anchor seining
II. Fly dragging

SENNE
Senne de fond
Eglefin, merlan, morue
Ecosse
I.  Pêche à l'ancre
II. Pêche en route

RED DE TIRO
Chinchorro fondero
Eglefino, merlán, bacalao
Escocia
I.  Pesca con ancla
II. Pesca en marcha

REFERENCE
W. Stewart
13 Dunbar Street
Lossiemouth, Morayshire
Scotland

VESSEL  BATEAU  BARCO

| Loa | Lht | Et | 13-15 m |
|-----|-----|-----|---------|
| GT  | TJB | TB | 20-40   |
| hp  | ch  | cv | 110-150 |

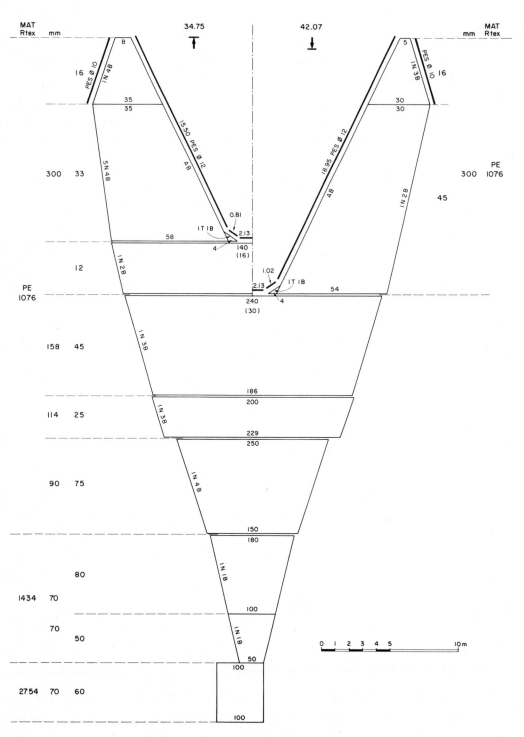

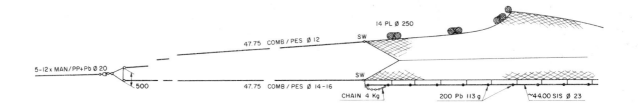

14 PL Ø 250

47.75   COMB / PES  Ø 12

SW

5-12 x MAN / PP+Pb Ø 20

500

47.75   COMB / PES  Ø 14-16

SW

CHAIN  4 Kg

200 Pb 113 g

~44.00 SIS  Ø 23

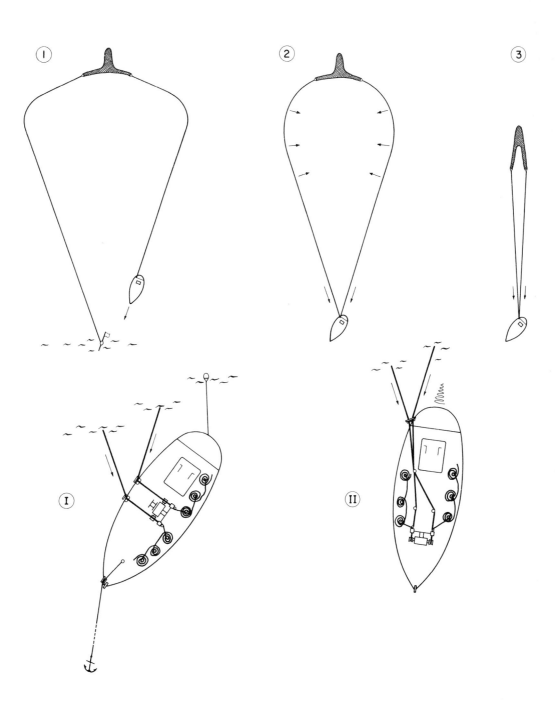

63

Bottom seine ("pair seine"), two-boat
Bottom fishes
Canada

SENNE
Senne de fond, à deux bateaux
Poissons de fond
Canada

RED DE TIRO
Chinchorro fondero, con dos barcos
Peces de fondo
Canadá

REFERENCE
Capt. J. Thomson
Allanfern, Stotfield Road
Lossiemouth, Morayshire
Scotland

| VESSEL | BATEAU | BARCO X 2 | |
|---|---|---|---|
| Loa | Lht | Et | 12 m |
| GT | TJB | TB | - |
| hp | ch | cv | 100-120 |

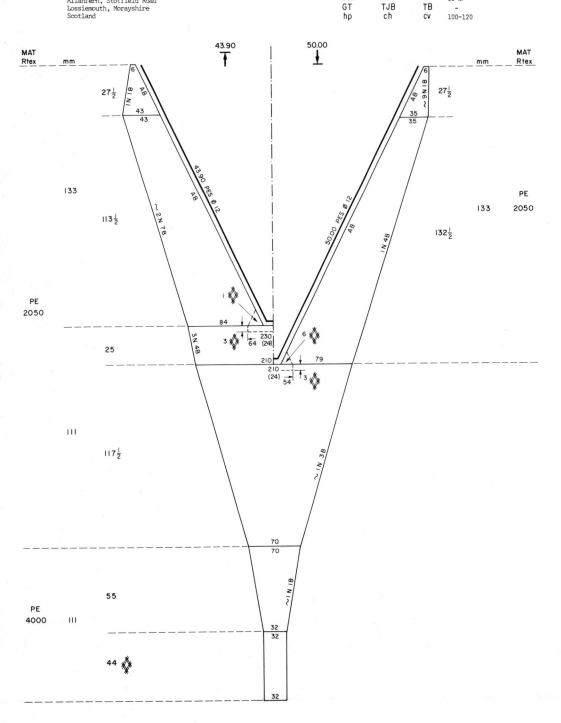

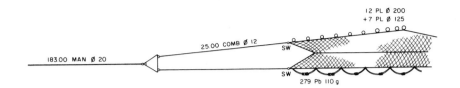

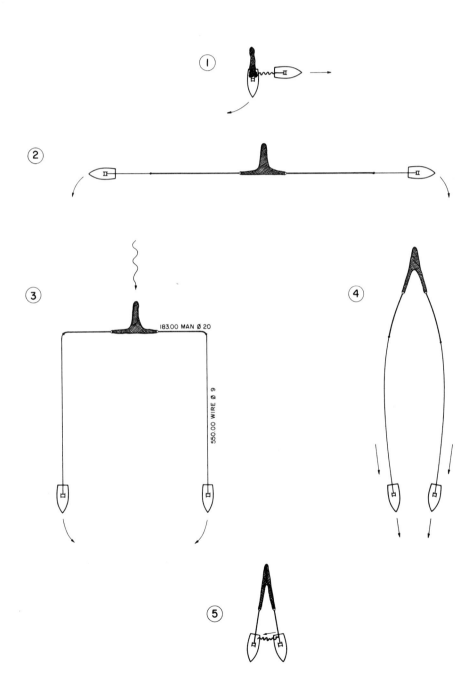

# TRAWL

Bottom, beam, double rig
Shrimp
E. and S. China Sea, Yellow Sea
Taiwan , China

# CHALUT

De fond, à perche, gréement double
Crevette
Mer de Chine E. et S., Mer Jaune
Taiwan , Chine

# RED DE ARRASTRE

De fondo, de vara, aparejo doble
Camarón
Mar de China E. y S., Mar Amarillo
Taiwán, China

REFERENCE
A.v. Brandt (after Tsann-Jun Lee)
Karlestrasse, 32
2 Hamburg 76, Fed. Rep. of Germany

| VESSEL | BATEAU | BARCO | |
|---|---|---|---|
| Loa | Lht | Et | 6-18 m |
| GT | TJB | TB | 5-10 |
| hp | ch | cv | 30-45 |

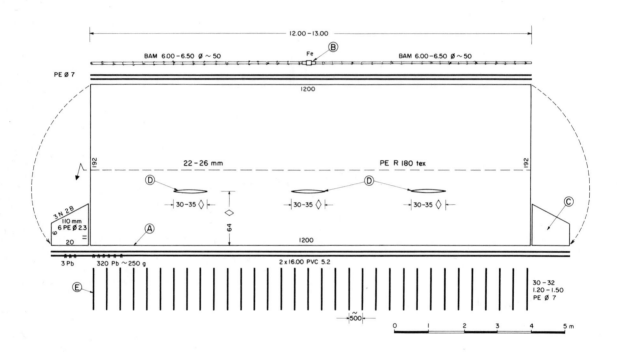

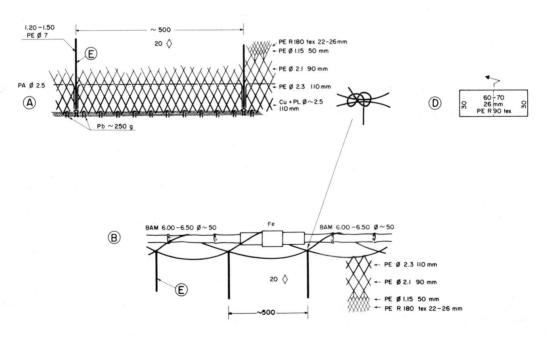

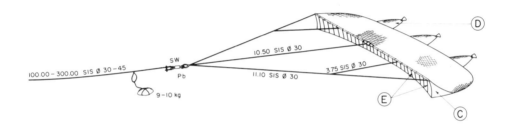

100.00 – 300.00  SIS Ø 30 – 45

SW

Pb

9 – 10 kg

10.50  SIS Ø 30

11.10  SIS Ø 30

3.75 SIS Ø 30

D

E

C

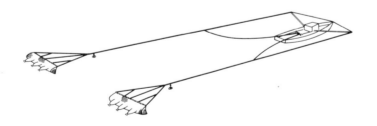

# TRAWL
Bottom, beam
Flatfish
United Kingdom

# CHALUT
De fond, à perche
Poissons plats
Royaume-Uni

# RED DE ARRASTRE
De fondo, de vara
Peces planos
Reino Unido

REFERENCE
H. Buckingham
(by courtesy: World Fishing, February/March 1973)

VESSEL  BATEAU  BARCO

| | | | |
|---|---|---|---|
| Loa | Lht | Et | 10-12 m |
| GT | TJB | TB | - |
| hp | ch | cv | 20-50 |

MAT
R tex    mm

3.60  PP Ø 10

96

~4.80  FAC

0.70   3

~4.20

~1.80 COMB Ø 12

~1.80 COMB Ø 12

4B

1.20

3  PA/PP Ø 8

MAT
mm    R tex

28

34

3 N 2B

Ⓐ

80

24        24

80
(32)

IN 4B

3 N 2B

PA
700-870    70

PA/PP Ø 8

PA
70    700-870

38

IN 4B

38

(30)

30
25

10

30

30

(25)

20
20

5

30

IN 2B

30

Ⓐ

20

870-1315  70  25

25  70  870-1315

0    1    2    3 m

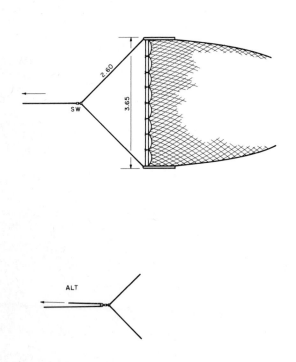

2.60

3.65

SW

ALT

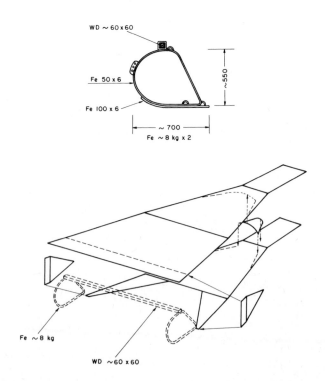

WD ~60 x 60

~550

Fe 50 x 6

Fe 100 x 6

~700

Fe ~8 kg x 2

Fe ~8 kg

WD ~60 x 60

**68**

# TRAWL

Bottom, beam ("plumb staff type")
Shrimp
Alaska, U.S.A.
British Columbia, Canada

# CHALUT

De fond, à perche
Crevette
Alaska, E.U.
Colombie Britannique, Canada

# RED DE ARRASTRE

De fondo, de vara
Camarón
Alaska, EE.UU.
Colombia Británica, Canadá

## REFERENCE

R.N. McBride
National Marine Fisheries Service
Kodiak, Alaska, U.S.A.

A.K. Larssen
Seattle, Washington, U.S.A.

J. Nomura
Stevenson, B.C., Canada

| VESSEL | BATEAU | BARCO | |
|--------|--------|-------|--------|
| Loa | Lht | Et | 10-15 m |
| GT | TJB | TB | 5-40 |
| hp | ch | cv | 100-150 |

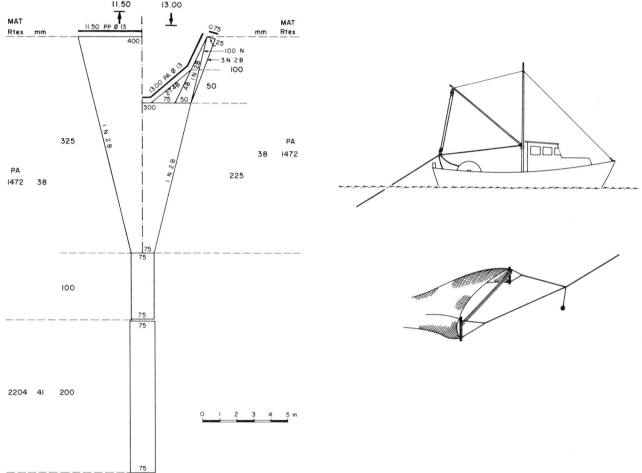

11.50    13.00

MAT
Rtex    mm

11.50 PP Ø 13
400
0.75
25
100 N
3 N 2 B
100
13.00 PA Ø 13
2 74B
AB I N 2B
50
75    50
300
mm    MAT
Rtex

1 N 2 B

325

1 N 2 B

PA
38    1472

225

PA
1472    38

75
75

100

75
75

2204    41    200

0   1   2   3   4   5 m

75

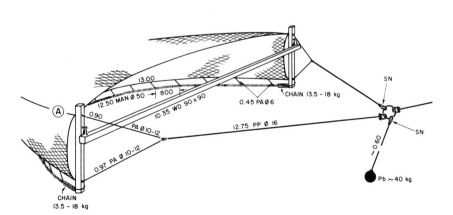

13.00
12.50 MAN Ø 50
800
0.45 PA Ø 6
CHAIN 13.5 - 18 kg
SN
10.35 WD 90 x 90
A
0.90
PA Ø 10-12
12.75 PP Ø 16
SN
0.97 PA Ø 10-12
0.60
CHAIN
13.5 - 18 kg
Pb ~ 40 kg

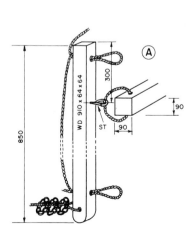

A
300
WD 910 x 64 x 64
90
850
ST
90

**69**

# TRAWL
Bottom, otter
Shrimp
Madagascar
I.  Soft ground
II. Hard ground

# CHALUT
De fond, à panneaux
Crevette
Madagascar
I.  Fond mou
II. Fond dur

# RED DE ARRASTRE
De fondo, con puertas
Camarón
Madagascar
I.  Fondo suave
II. Fondo duro

REFERENCE
J.B. Prat, G. Nédélec, D. Razafindrakoto
Direction de l'Elevage et de la Pêche Maritime
Madagascar

| VESSEL | BATEAU | BARCO | |
|---|---|---|---|
| Loa | Lht | Et | 7.30 m |
| GT | TJB | TB | - |
| hp | ch | cv | 14-25 |

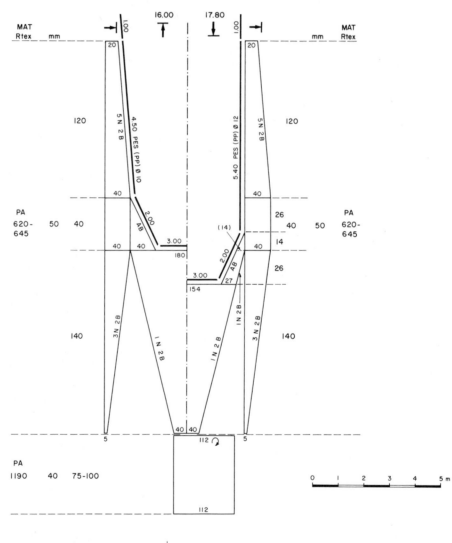

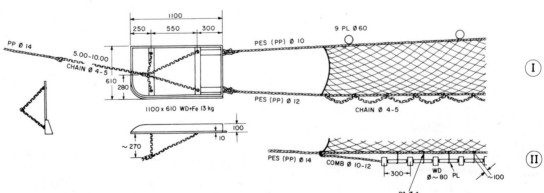

I

II

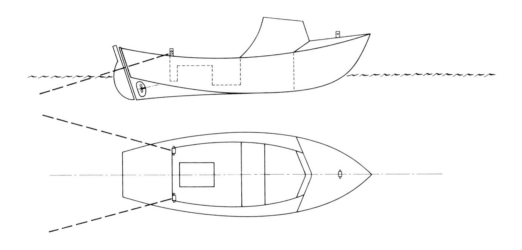

# TRAWL
Bottom, otter
Shrimp
Cochin, India

# CHALUT
De fond, à panneaux
Crevette
Cochin, Inde

# RED DE ARRASTRE
De fondo, con puertas
Camarón
Cochin, India

**REFERENCE**
V.K. Pillai
Central Institute of Fisheries Technology
Ernakulam, Cochin
India

| VESSEL | BATEAU | BARCO | I | II |
|--------|--------|-------|------|------|
| Loa | Lht | Et | 9.15 m | 10.95 m |
| GT | TJB | TB | - | - |
| hp | ch | cv | 30 | 60-80 |

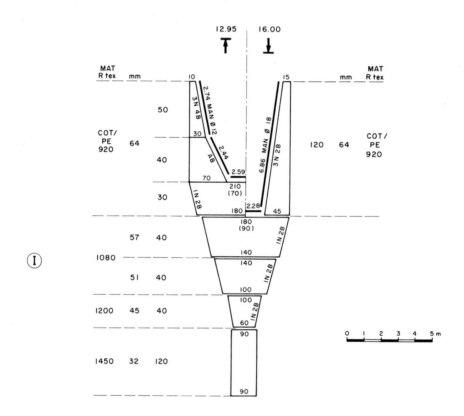

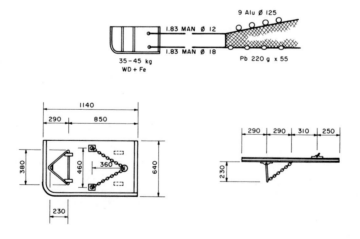

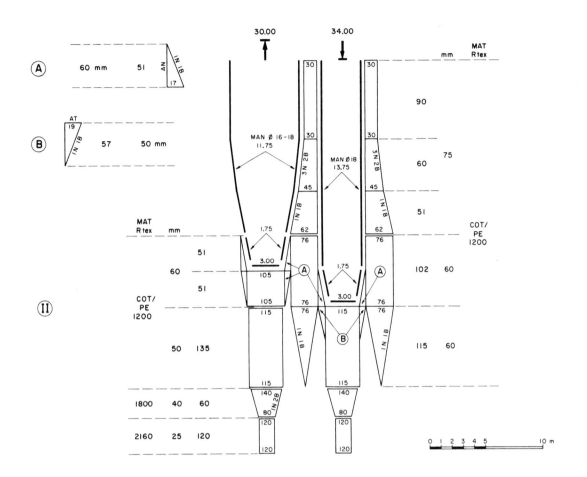

(A)  60 mm  51  AN IN 1B  17

(B)  AT 19 IN 1B  57  50 mm

(II)

30.00 ↑     34.00 ↓

MAT mm Rtex

MAN Ø 16-18 11.75     MAN Ø 18 13.75

30
30
30
30
3N 2B
3N 2B
45
45
IN 1B
IN 1B
62
62
76
76

90
75
60
51

COT/ PE 1200

MAT Rtex mm

51
60
51
COT/ PE 1200
50  135

1.75
3.00
105
(A)
105
115
IN 1B

1.75
3.00
76
76
(A)
115
115
140
IN 2B
80
120
120

102  60
115  60

1800  40  60
2160  25  120

140
80
120
120

0 1 2 3 4 5 ___ 10 m

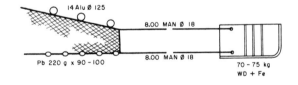

14 Alu Ø 125
8.00 MAN Ø 18
Pb 220 g x 90-100
8.00 MAN Ø 18
70 - 75 kg WD + Fe

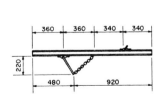

360  360  340  340
220
480  920

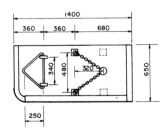

1400
360  360  680
650
340  480  320
250

73

# TRAWL
Bottom, otter
Flatfish
E. English Channel, France

# CHALUT
De fond, à panneaux
Poissons plats
Manche E., France

# RED DE ARRASTRE
De fondo, con puertas
Peces planos
Canal de la Mancha E., Francia

## REFERENCE
L. Libert
Institut des Pêches Maritimes
Boulogne-sur-Mer, France

VESSEL  BATEAU  BARCO

| Loa | Lht | Et | 6 m |
|-----|-----|-----|-----|
| GT | TJB | TB | - |
| hp | ch | cv | 20 |

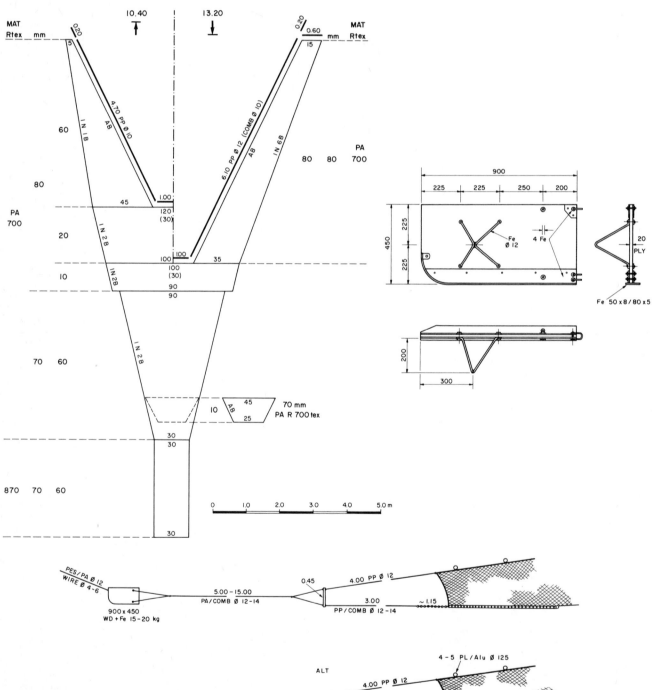

Fe 50 x 8 / 80 x 5

PES/PA Ø 12
WIRE Ø 4-6

900 x 450
WD + Fe 15-20 kg

5.00 - 15.00
PA/COMB Ø 12-14

0.45

4.00 PP Ø 12

~1.15

3.00
PP/COMB Ø 12-14

ALT

4.00 PP Ø 12

4-5 PL/Alu Ø 125

~1.15

3.00
PP/COMB Ø 12-14

1 kg/m

2-4 kg/m

74

# TRAWL
Bottom, otter
Bottom species
E. English Channel, France

# CHALUT
De fond, à panneaux
Espèces de fond
Manche E., France

# RED DE ARRASTRE
De fondo, con puertas
Especies de fondo
Canal de la Mancha E., Francia

## REFERENCE
M. Portier
Institut des Pêches Maritimes
Boulogne-sur-Mer, France

## VESSEL BATEAU BARCO

| Loa | Lht | Et | 8-10 m |
|-----|-----|-----|--------|
| GT | TJB | TB | - |
| hp | ch | cv | 50 |

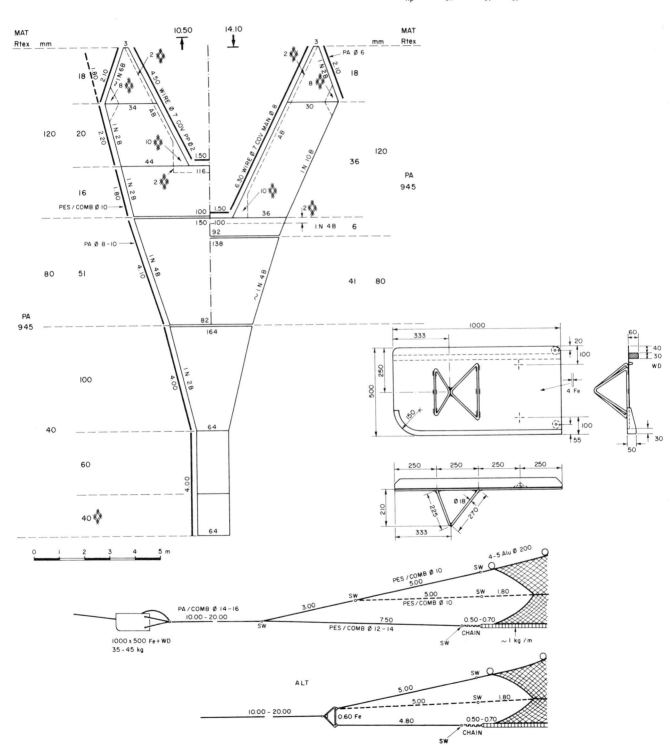

# TRAWL
Bottom, otter
Herring
Baltic, Poland

# CHALUT
De fond, à panneaux
Hareng
Baltique, Pologne

# RED DE ARRASTRE
De fondo, con puertas
Arenque
Báltico, Polonia

REFERENCE
S. Prüffer, J. Kucyszyn, J. Rogozinski, W. Strzyzewski
Fishing Gear Department
Fisheries Central Board
Szczecin, Poland

| VESSEL | BATEAU | BARCO | |
|--------|--------|-------|------|
| Loa | Lht | Et | 17 m |
| GT | TJB | TB | 36 |
| hp | ch | cv | 120 |

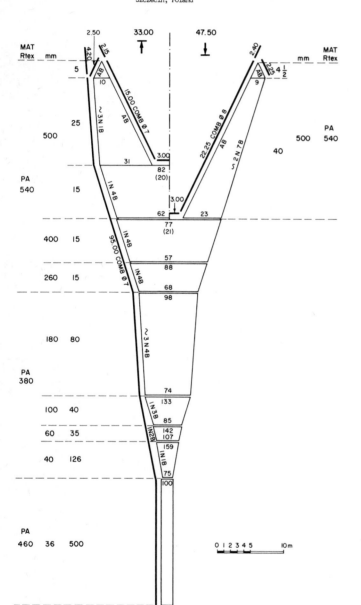

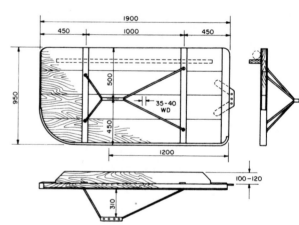

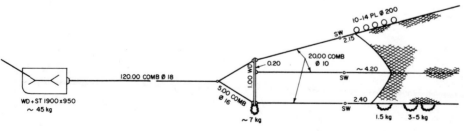

# TRAWL

Bottom, otter
Rough bottom
Cod
Baltic, Fed. Rep. of Germany

# CHALUT

De fond, à panneaux
Fond dur
Morue
Baltique, Rép. Féd. d'Allemagne

# RED DE ARRASTRE

De fondo, con puertas
Fondo duro
Bacalao
Báltico, Rep. Fed. de Alemania

## REFERENCE

Institut für Fangtechnik
2000 Hamburg 50, Palmaille 9
Fed. Rep. of Germany

| VESSEL | BATEAU | BARCO | |
|--------|--------|-------|------------|
| Loa | Lht | Et | 12–18 m |
| GT | TJB | TB | 25–40 |
| hp | ch | cv | 100–150 |

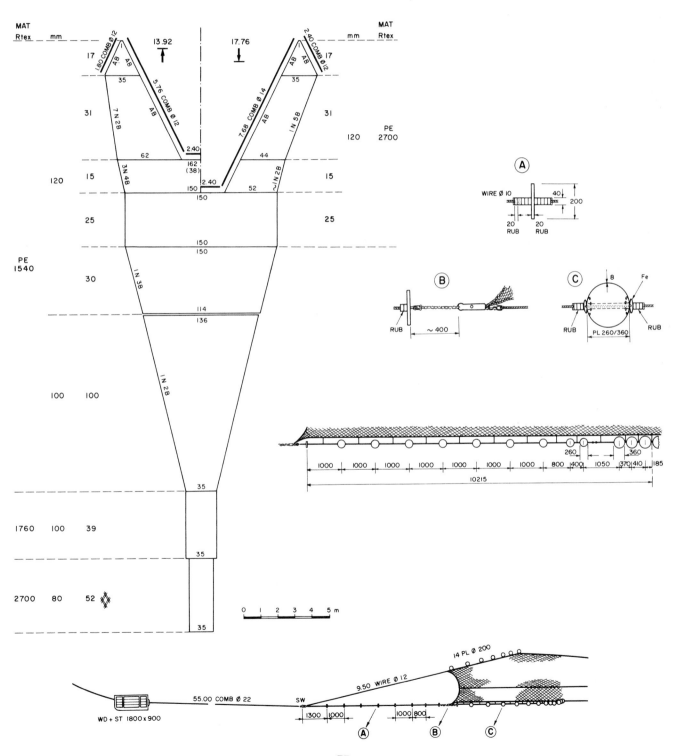

77

# TRAWL
Bottom, pair
I. Miscellaneous species
II. Eel
Inshore; lakes and rivers
Fed. Rep. of Germany

# CHALUT
De fond, chalut-boeuf
I. Espèces diverses
II. Anguille
Côtier; lacs et fleuves
Rép. Féd. d'Allemagne

# RED DE ARRASTRE
De fondo, pareja
I. Especies diversas
II. Anguila
Costero; lagos y ríos
Rep. Fed. de Alemania

**REFERENCE**
R. Steinberg
Institut für Fangtechnik
2000 Hamburg 50, Palmaille 9
Fed. Rep. of Germany

| VESSEL | BATEAU | BARCO | x 2 |
|--------|--------|-------|-----|
| Loa | Lht | Et | 5-6 m |
| GT | TJB | TB | - |
| hp | ch | cv | 15-20 |

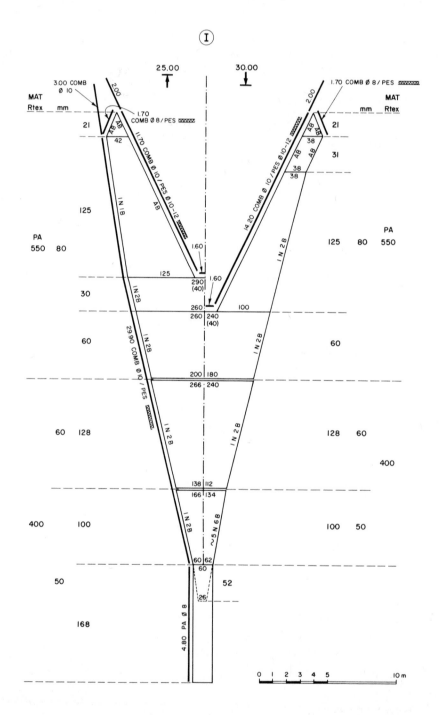

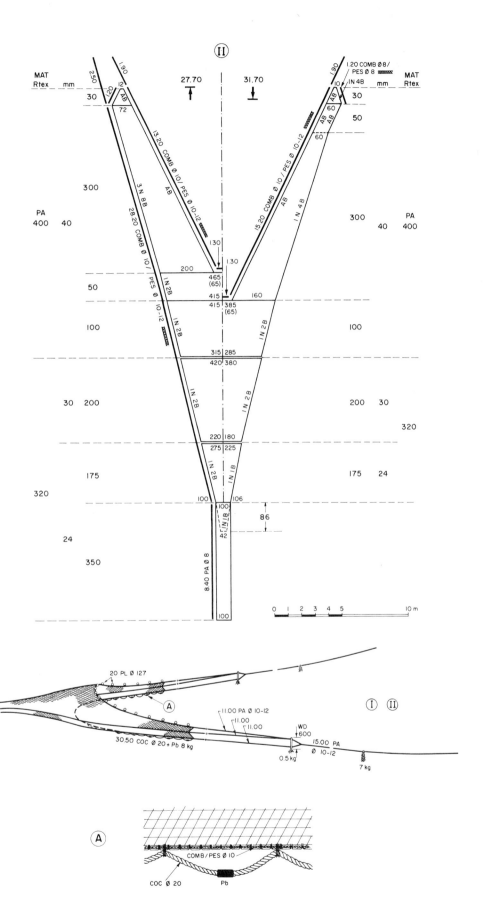

79

TRAWL
Bottom, pair
Freshwater fishes
Lake Chilwa, Malawi

CHALUT
De fond, chalut-boeuf
Poissons d'eau douce
Lac Chilwa, Malawi

RED DE ARRASTRE
De fondo, pareja
Peces de agua dulce
Lago Chilwa, Malawi

REFERENCE
C. Ratcliffe
Ministry of Agriculture and Natural Resources
Zomba, Malawi

H. Buckingham (in: World Fishing)

| VESSEL | BATEAU | BARCO | X 2 |
|--------|--------|-------|-----|
| Loa | Lht | Et | 5 m |
| GT | TJB | TB | - |
| hp | ch | cv | 4-5 |

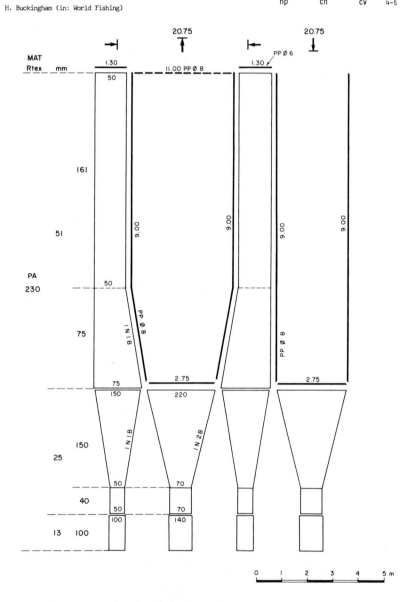

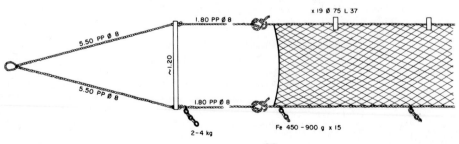

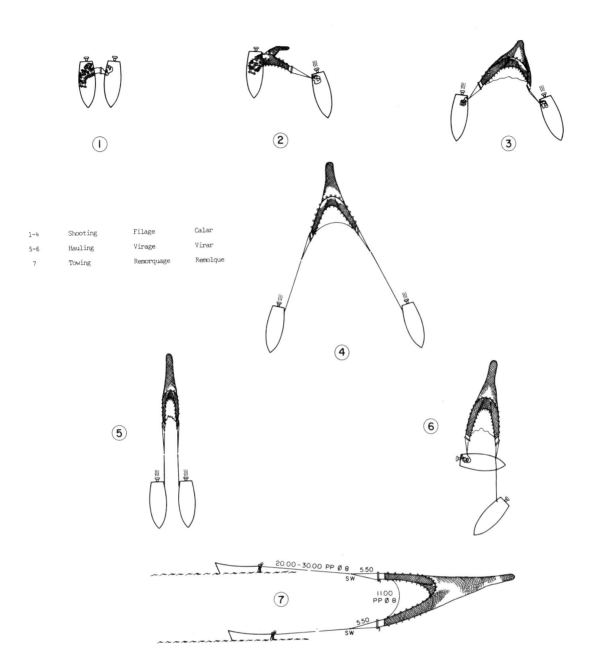

| 1-4 | Shooting | Filage | Calar |
| 5-6 | Hauling | Virage | Virar |
| 7 | Towing | Remorquage | Remolque |

20.00 - 30.00 PP Ø 8    5.50
SW
11.00
PP Ø 8
5.50
SW

TRAWL
Midwater, otter
Sprat, anchovy, sardine
S. Brittany, France

CHALUT
Pélagique, à panneaux
Sprat, anchois, sardine
Bretagne S., France

RED DE ARRASTRE
Pelágica, con puertas
Espadín, anchoa, sardina
Bretaña S., Francia

REFERENCE
M. Portier
Institut des Pêches Maritimes
Boulogne-sur-Mer, France

L. Le Pape
Le Croisic, France

VESSEL  BATEAU  BARCO

| Loa | Lht | Et | 15 m |
|-----|-----|-----|------|
| GT | TJB | TB | 35 |
| hp | ch | cv | 150 |

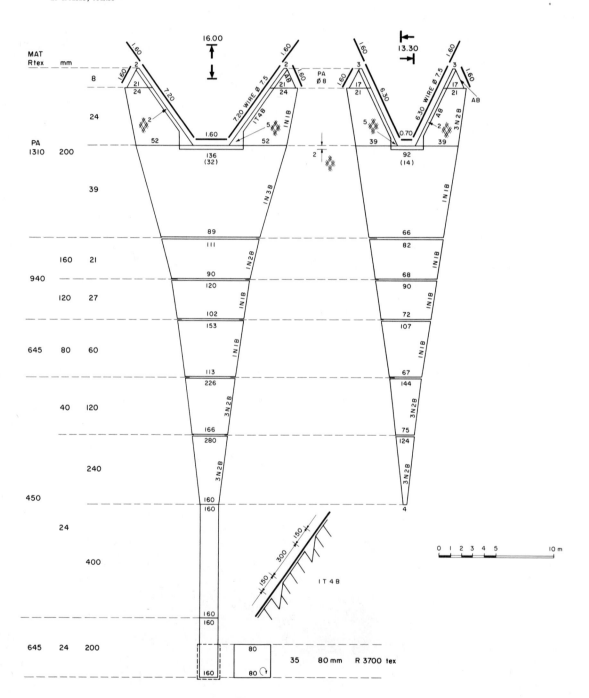

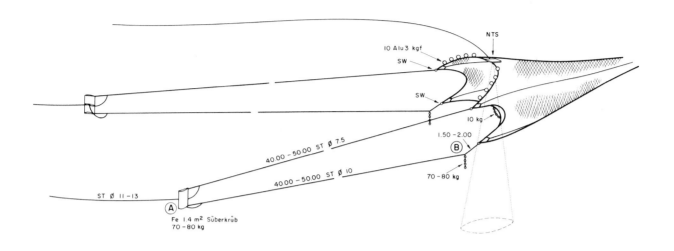

NTS

10 Alu 3 kgf

SW

SW

10 kg

1.50 - 2.00

Ⓑ

70 - 80 kg

40.00 - 50.00 ST Ø 7.5

40.00 - 50.00 ST Ø 10

ST Ø 11-13

Ⓐ

Fe 1.4 m² Süberkrüb
70 - 80 kg

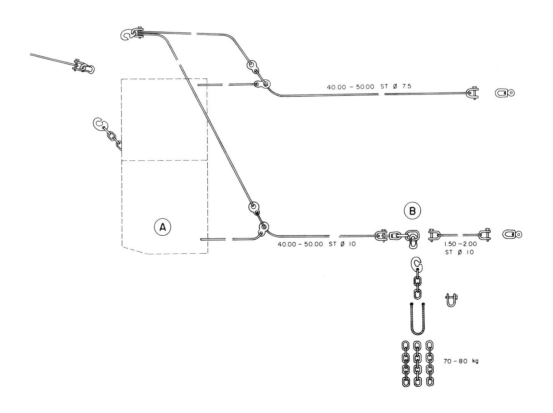

40.00 - 50.00 ST Ø 7.5

Ⓐ

Ⓑ

40.00 - 50.00 ST Ø 10

1.50 - 2.00
ST Ø 10

70 - 80 kg

# TRAWL
Midwater, pair
Herring, cod, whiting
E. English Channel, France

# CHALUT
Pélagique, chalut-boeuf
Hareng, morue, merlan
Manche E., France

# RED DE ARRASTRE
Pelágica, con puertas
Arenque, bacalao, merlán
Canal de la Mancha E., Francia

### REFERENCE
M. Portier
Institut des Pêches Maritimes
Boulogne-sur-Mer, France

VESSEL  BATEAU  BARCO  X 2

| | | | |
|---|---|---|---|
| Loa | Lht | Et | 6 m |
| GT | TJB | TB | – |
| hp | ch | cv | 9-15 |

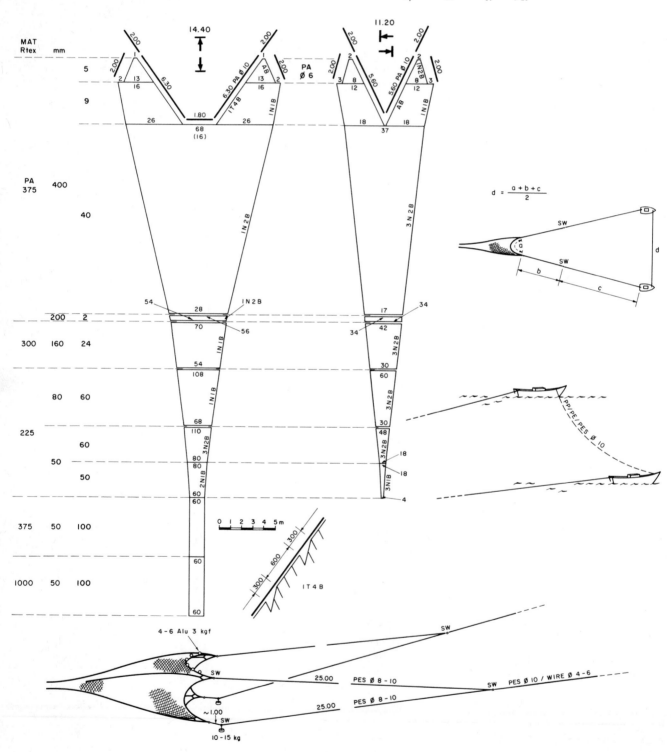

$$d = \frac{a+b+c}{2}$$

84

## TRAWL
Midwater, pair
Herring, sprat
Baltic, Poland

## CHALUT
Pélagique, chalut-boeuf
Hareng, sprat
Baltique, Pologne

## RED DE ARRASTRE
Pelágica, pareja
Arenque, espadín
Báltico, Polonia

REFERENCE
J. Kucyszyn, S. Prüffer, W. Strzyzewski
Fishing Gear Department
Fisheries Central Board
Szczecin, Poland

| VESSEL | BATEAU | BARCO | X 2 |
|--------|--------|-------|------|
| Loa | Lht | Et | 17 m |
| GT | TJB | TB | 36 |
| hp | ch | cv | 120 |

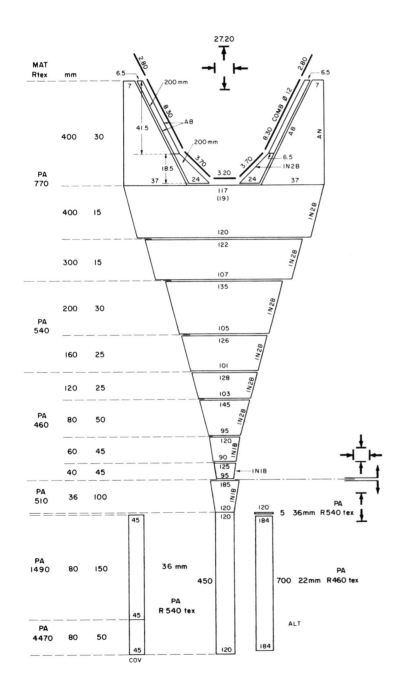

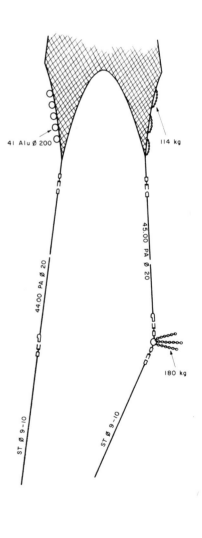

0  2  4  6  8  10 m

85

# TRAWL
Midwater, pair
Freshwater fishes
Lakes, Rep. Fed. of Germany

# CHALUT
Pélagique, chalut-boeuf
Poissons d'eau douce
Lacs, Rép. Fed. d'Allemagne

# RED DE ARRASTRE
Pelágica, pareja
Peces de agua dulce
Lagos, Rep. Fed. de Alemania

**REFERENCE**
R. Steinberg, E. Dahm
Institut für Fangtechnik
2000 Hamburg 50, Pailmaille 9
Fed. Rep. of Germany

| VESSEL | BATEAU | BARCO | X 2 |
|--------|--------|-------|------|
| Loa | Lht | Et | 5-6 m |
| GT | TJB | TB | - |
| hp | ch | cv | 20 |

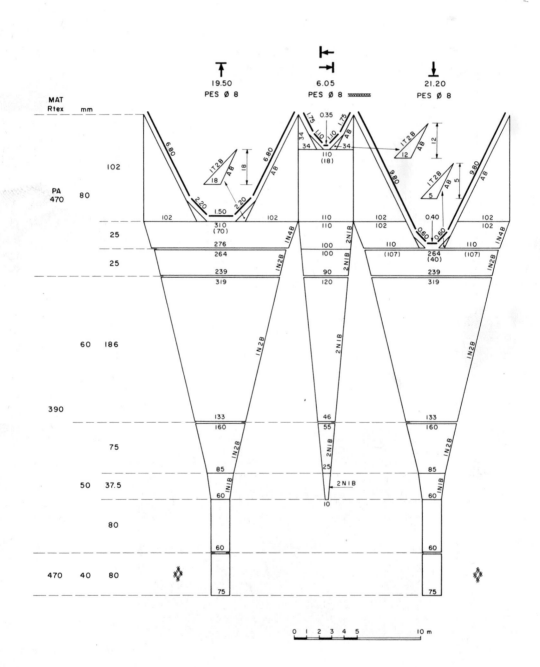

0 1 2 3 4 5        10 m

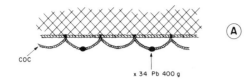

COC

x 34 Pb 400 g

(A)

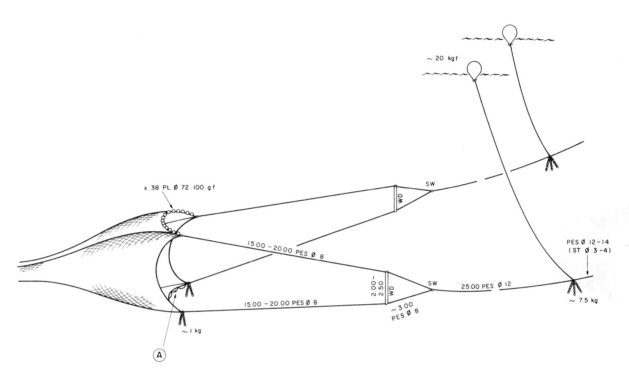

x 38 PL Ø 72 100 g f

15.00 – 20.00 PES Ø 8

15.00 – 20.00 PES Ø 8

WD

SW

WD

SW

2.00 – 2.50

~ 3.00 PES Ø 8

25.00 PES Ø 12

PES Ø 12–14 (ST Ø 3 –4)

~ 20 kgf

~ 7.5 kg

~ 1 kg

(A)

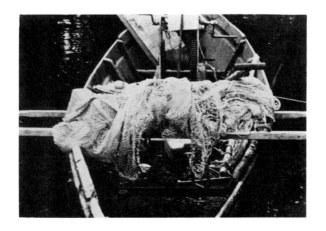

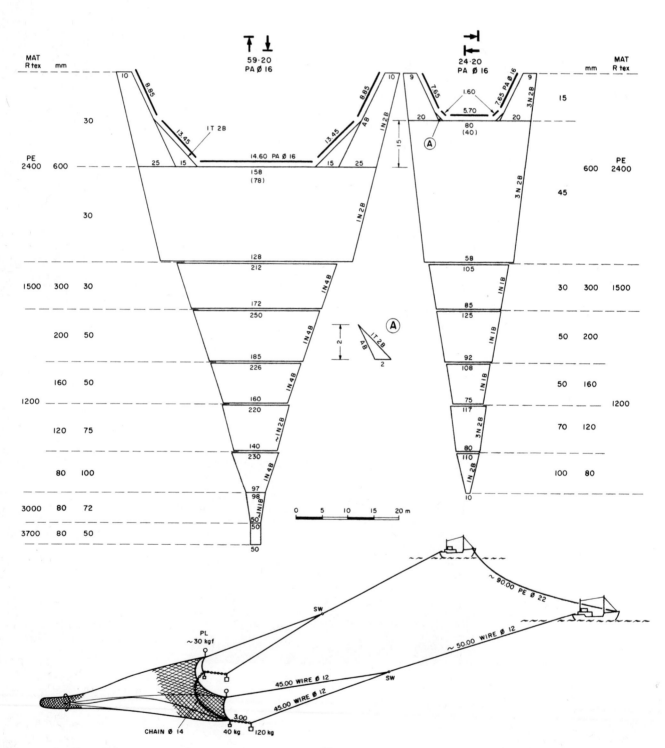

**TRAWL**
Midwater, pair
Cod, whiting
S. North Sea, Belgium

**CHALUT**
Pélagique, chalut-boeuf
Morue, merlan
Mer du Nord S, Belgique

**RED DE ARRASTRE**
Pelágica, pareja
Bacalao, merlán
Mar del Norte S., Bélgica

**REFERENCE**
G. Van den Broucke
Rijksstation voor Zeevisserij
Oostende, Belgique

| VESSEL | BATEAU | BARCO | X 2 |
|--------|--------|-------|------|
| Loa | Lht | Et | 14 m |
| GT | TJB | TB | 30-40 |
| hp | ch | cv | 150 |

59·20
PA Ø 16

24·20
PA Ø 16

88

# DREDGE

Boat-operated
Murex
Mediterranean, France

# DRAGUE

Manoeuvrée du bateau
Murex
Méditerranée, France

# RASTRO

Maniobrada desde el barco
Murex
Mediterráneo, Francia

REFERENCE

P.Y. Dremière (d'après Albanez)
Institut des Pêches Maritimes
Sète, France

| VESSEL | BATEAU | BARCO | |
|--------|--------|-------|--------|
| Loa | Lht | Et | 8-13 m |
| GT | TJB | TB | – |
| hp | ch | cv | 50-100 |

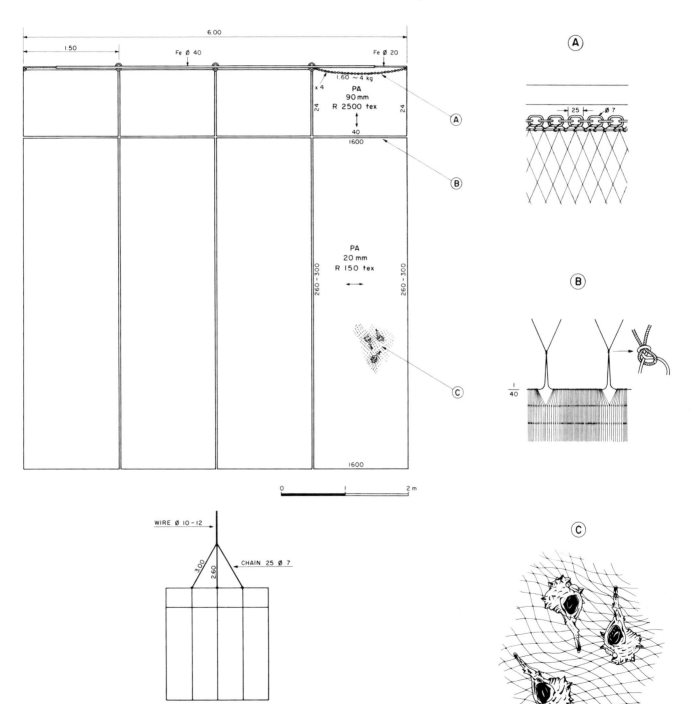

**89**

## DREDGE
Boat-operated
Scallop
Australia

## DRAGUE
Manoeuvrée du bateau
Coquille St. Jacques
Australie

## RASTRO
Maniobrada desde el barco
Vieiras
Australia

**REFERENCE**
W.D. Hughes
Fisheries Division, Department of Primary Industry
Canberra, Australia

| VESSEL | BATEAU | BARCO | |
|--------|--------|-------|--------|
| Loa | Lht | Et | 9-15 m |
| GT | TJB | TB | - |
| hp | ch | cv | 70-150 |

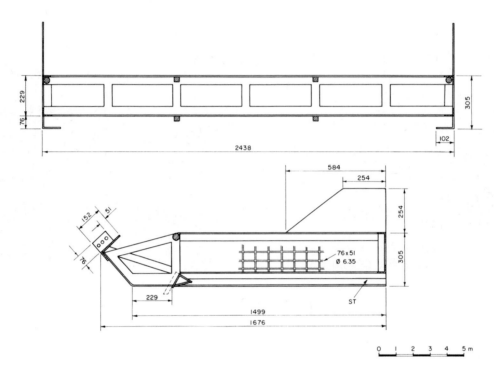

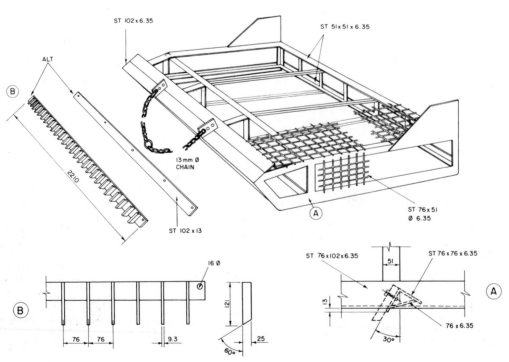

ST 102 x 6.35

ST 51 x 51 x 6.35

ALT

13 mm Ø
CHAIN

ST 102 x 13

2210

ST 76 x 51
Ø 6.35

B

16 Ø

76    76    9.3

121    25    60°

ST 76 x 102 x 6.35    ST 76 x 76 x 6.35

51    13    76 x 6.35    30°

A

90

# LIFTNET
Portable
Elver (young eel)
Adour, S.W. France

# FILET SOULEVE
Transportable
Civelle (jeune anguille)
Adour, France S.-0.

# RED IZADA
Portátil
Anguila juvenil
Adour, Francia S.-0.

REFERENCE

A. Percier
Centre d'études et de recherches scientifiques
Biarritz, France

| VESSEL | BATEAU | BARCO | FAC |
|--------|--------|-------|-----|
| Loa | Lht | Et | |
| GT | TJB | TB | |
| hp | ch | cv | |

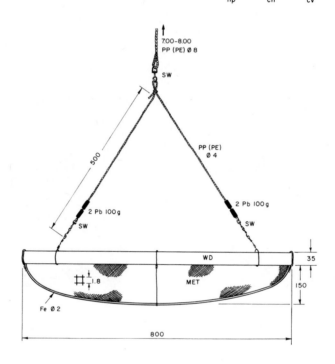

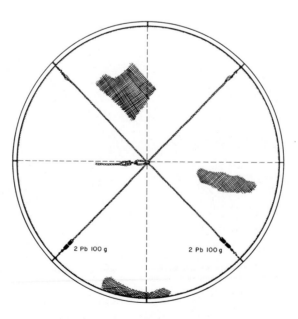

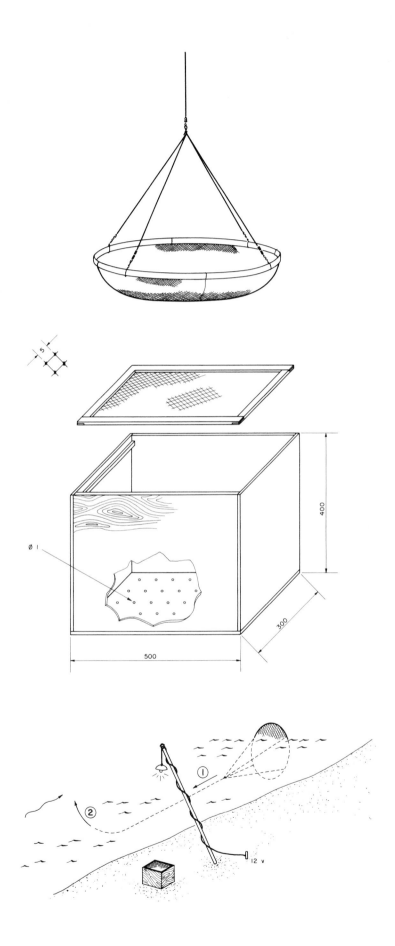

Ø 1

400

300

500

5

① ② 12 v

# LIFTNET
Portable
Crab
Philippines

# FILET SOULEVE
Transportable
Crabe
Philippines

# RED IZADA
Portátil
Cangrejo
Filipinas

### REFERENCE
A. v. Brandt (after Ming-Yong Chen)
Karlestrasse, 32
2 Hamburg 76, Fed.Rep. of Germany

VESSEL BATEAU BARCO     FAC

| Loa | Lht | Et |
|-----|-----|-----|
| GT  | TJB | TB |
| hp  | ch  | cv |

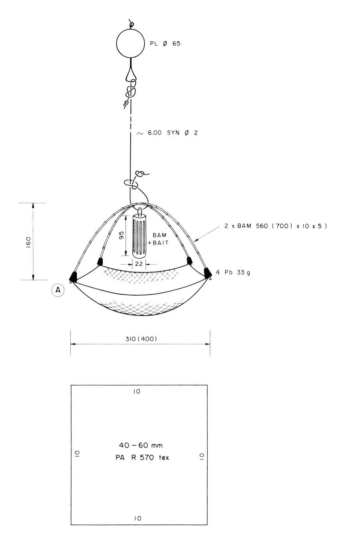

PL Ø 65

~ 6.00 SYN Ø 2

2 x BAM 560 (700) x 10 x 5)

BAM + BAIT

160

95

22

4 Pb 33 g

310 (400)

10

10

10

10

40 – 60 mm
PA R 570 tex

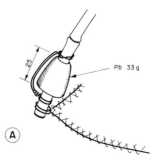

25

Pb 33 g

Ⓐ

LIFTNET

Boat-operated
Ndagala
Lake Tanganyika, Burundi
I    Smaller version, for catamaran
II   Larger version, for trimaran

FILET SOULEVE

Manoeuvré du bateau
Ndagala
Lac Tanganika, Burundi
I    Petit modèle, pour catamaran
II   Grand modèle, pour trimaran

RED IZADA

Maniobrada desde el barco
Ndagala
Lago Tanganyika, Burundi
I    Modelo pequeño, para catamarán
II   Modelo grande, para trimarán

REFERENCE

A. Collart, L. Haling
FAO

| VESSEL | BATEAU | BARCO | X 2-3 |
|--------|--------|-------|-------|
| Loa | Lht | Et | 6 m |
| GT | TJB | TB | – |
| hp | ch | cv | 15 |

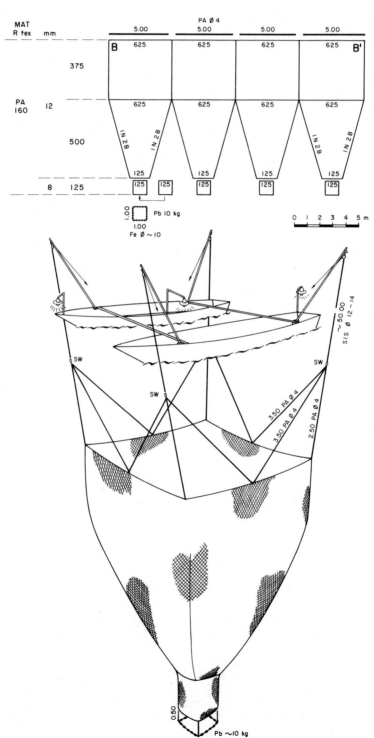

96

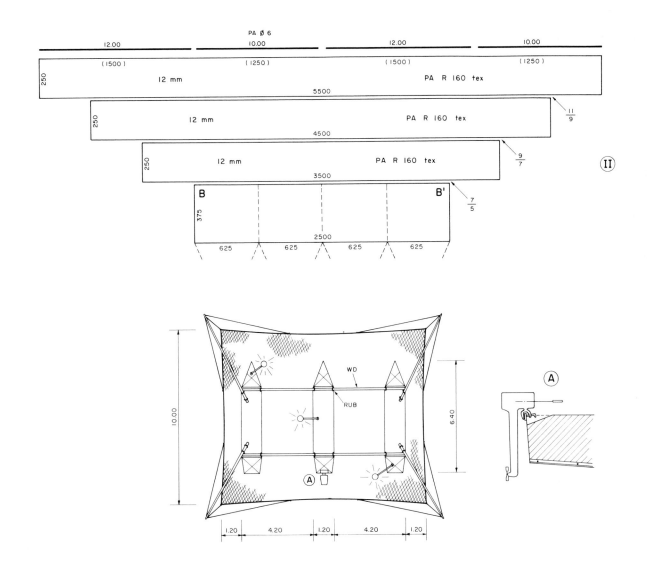

PA Ø 6

12.00       10.00       12.00       10.00

(1500)     (1250)     (1500)     (1250)

250     12 mm     PA R 160 tex

5500

$\frac{11}{9}$

250     12 mm     PA R 160 tex

4500

$\frac{9}{7}$

250     12 mm     PA R 160 tex

3500

$\frac{7}{5}$

(II)

B     B'

375

625    625    625    625

2500

WD

RUB

10.00     6.40

Ⓐ

1.20   4.20   1.20   4.20   1.20

Ⓐ

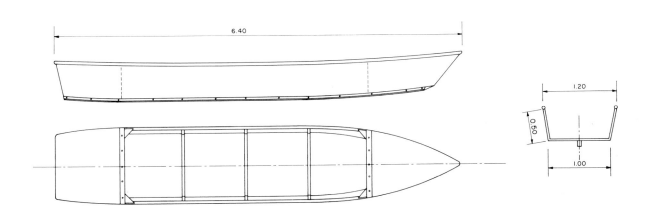

6.40

1.20

0.50

1.00

LIFTNET
Boat-operated
Stick-held dipnet (bouke-ami)
For catching live-bait
Pacific, Fiji Islands

FILET SOULEVE
Manoeuvré du bateau
Monté sur bâtons
Pour pêche d'appât vivant
Pacifique, Iles Fidji

RED IZADA
Maniobrada desde el barco
Con varas
Para pescar la carnada viva
Pacífico, Islas Fiji

REFERENCE
R.M. Stone
Fisheries Division
Lami, Suva, Fiji

R. Lee
FAO

| VESSEL | BATEAU | BARCO | |
|--------|--------|-------|------|
| Loa | Lht | Et | 15 m |
| GT | TJB | TB | – |
| hp | ch | cv | – |

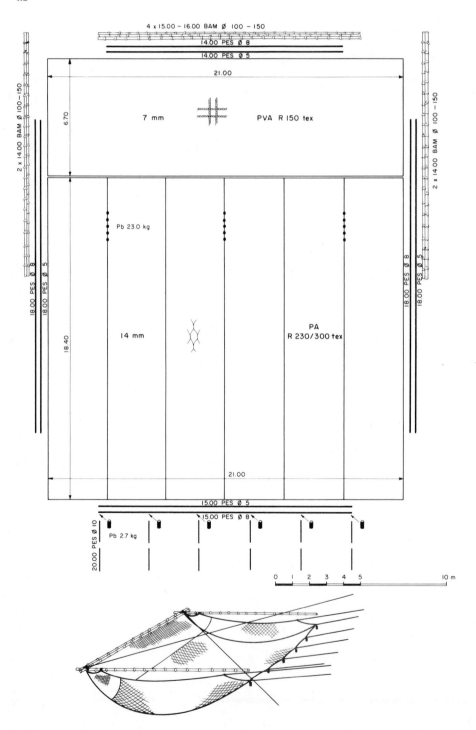

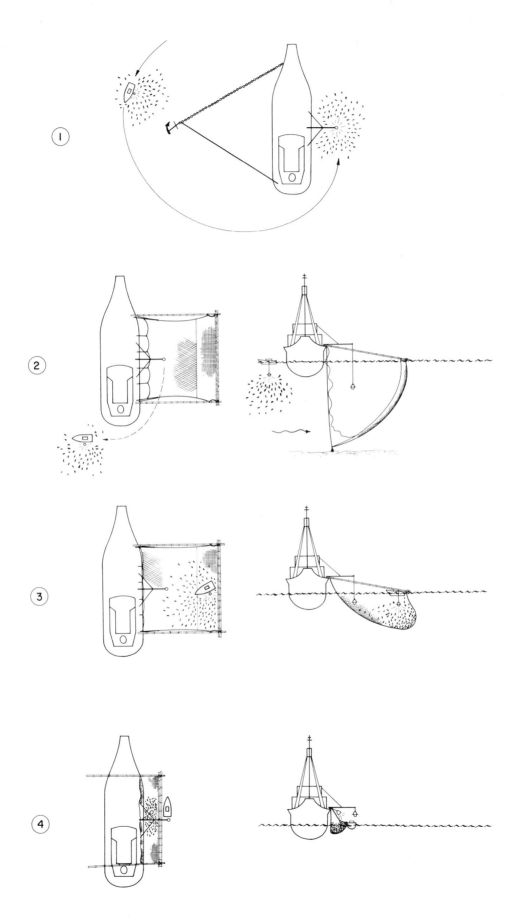

99

LIFTNET
Shore-operated, stationery
Mullets, clupeids, eel
Adriatic, Italy

FILET SOULEVE
Manoeuvré du rivage, fixe
Mulet, clupéïdes, anguille
Adriatique, Italie

RED IZADA
Maniobrada desde la costa, fija
Mujol, clupeidos, anguila
Adriático, Italia

REFERENCE
G. Bombace, B. Galli
Laboratorio de tecnologia della pesca
Ancona, Italy

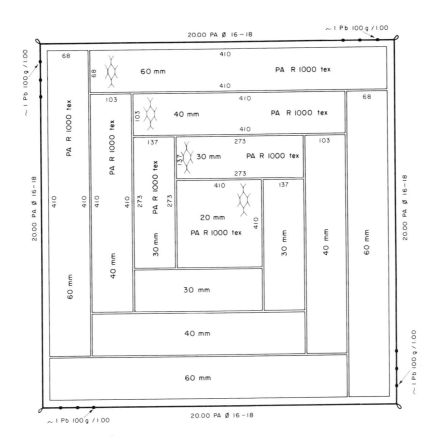

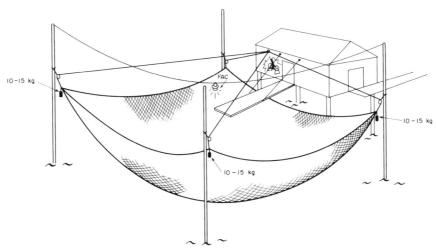

## LIFTNET
Shore-operated, stationery
Freshwater fishes
Danube, Rumania

## FILET SOULEVE
Manoeuvré du rivage, fixe
Poissons d'eau douce
Danube, Roumanie

## RED IZADA
Maniobrada desde la costa, fija
Peces de agua dulce
Danubio, Rumania

### REFERENCE
N. Bacalbasa-Dobrovici
Str. Partizanilor 29, ap. 51
Galati 6, Roumanie

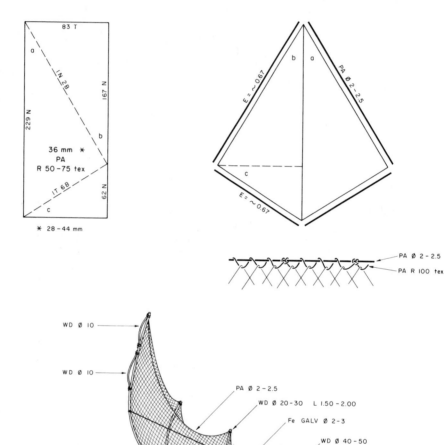

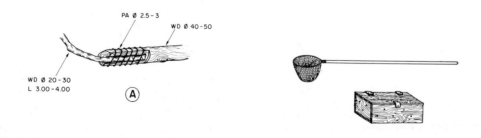

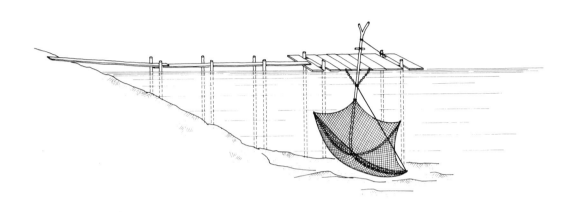

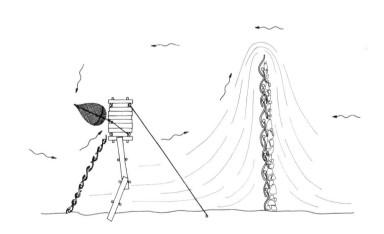

CASTNET
Hand
I  With pockets
II With closing lines
Mullet, ethmalosa (bonga), misc. species
Rivers, Senegal

EPERVIER
A main
I  Avec poches
II Avec fils de fermeture
Mulet, ethmalose, espèces diverses
Fleuves, Sénégal

ESPARAVEL
A mano
I  Con bolsillos
II Con hilos de cerradura
Mujol, ethmalosa, especies
   diversas
Ríos, Senegal

REFERENCE
P. Seck
c/o Direction de l'Océanographie et des Pêches
Dakar, Sénégal

| VESSEL | BATEAU | BARCO | FAC |
|--------|--------|-------|------|
| Loa | Lht | Et | 4-6 m |
| GT | TJB | TB | – |
| hp | ch | cv | – |

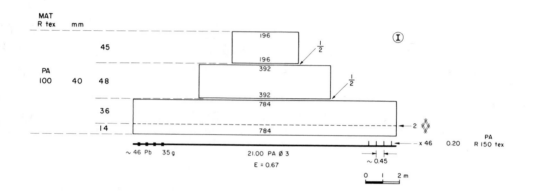

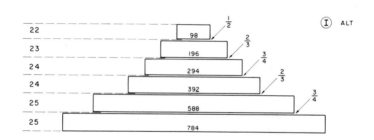

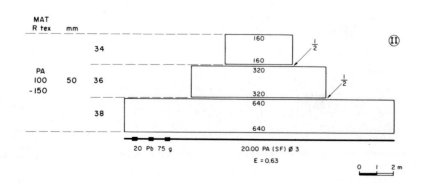

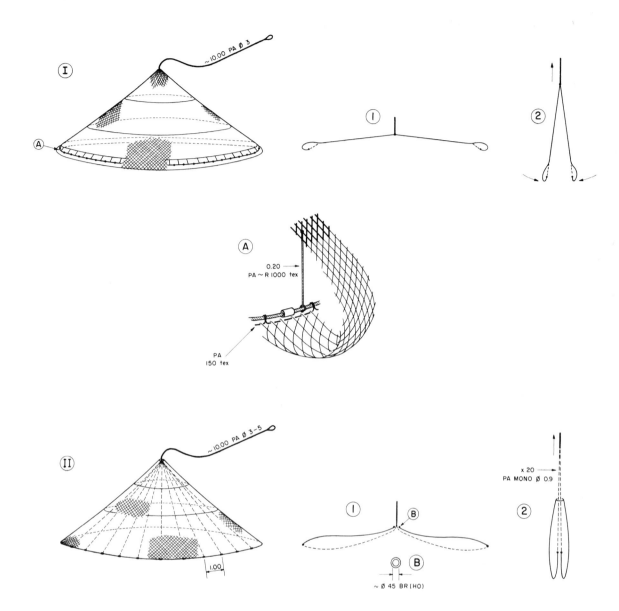

I

~10.00 PA Ø 3

A

1

2

A

0.20 →
PA ~ R 1000 tex

PA
150 tex

II

~10.00 PA Ø 3-5

1.00

1

B

B

~ Ø 45 BR (HO)

x 20 →
PA MONO Ø 0.9

2

# GILLNET

Bottom set
Roach, perch
Lakes
Fed. Rep. of Germany

# FILET MAILLANT

Calé sur le fond
Gardon, perche
Lacs
Rép. Féd. d'Allemagne

# RED DE ENMALLE

De fondo, calada
Bermejuela, perca
Lagos
Rep. Féd. de Alemania

## REFERENCE

M. Kaulin
Maxburgstrasse, 13
6735 Maikammer, Fed. Rep. of Germany

A. v. Brandt
Karlestrasse, 32
2 Hamburg 76, Fed. Rep. of Germany

VESSEL  BATEAU  BARCO

| Loa | Lht | Et | 5-7 m |
|-----|-----|-----|-------|
| GT | TJB | TB | - |
| hp | ch | cv | 3-20 |

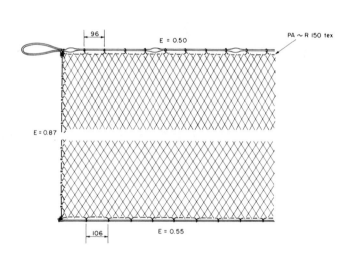

# GILLNET

Bottom set
Croakers
Senegal

# FILET MAILLANT

Calé sur le fond
Capitaines
Sénégal

# RED DE ENMALLE

De fondo, calada
Corbinas
Senegal

REFERENCE

P. Seck
c/o Direction de l'océanographie et des pêches
Dakar, Sénégal

VESSEL BATEAU BARCO

| | | | |
|---|---|---|---|
| Loa | Lht | Et | 7 m |
| GT | TJB | TB | - |
| hp | ch | cv | 6 |

90.00 PE (PP) Ø 6

| II | 140 mm | 900 900 | PA R 450 tex | II |

90.00 PE (PP) Ø 6

0 1 2 3 4 5    10 m

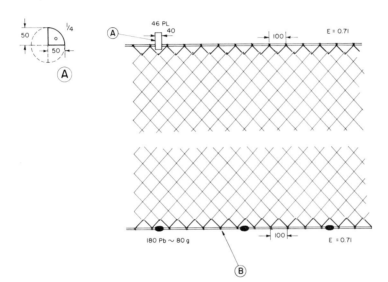

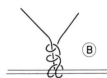

180 Pb ~ 80 g    100    E = 0.71

46 PL    40    100    E = 0.71

50    1/4    50

A

B

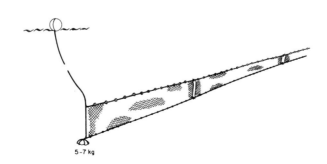

5 - 7 kg

**107**

# GILLNET
Bottom set
Cod, flounder
Newfoundland, Canada

# FILET MAILLANT
Calé sur le fond
Morue, poissons plats
Terre-Neuve, Canada

# RED DE ENMALLE
De fondo, calada
Bacalao, peces planos
Terranova, Canadá

### REFERENCE
A.J. Provan, R.G. Kingsley
College of Fisheries
St. John's, Newfoundland, Canada

| VESSEL | BATEAU | BARCO | |
|---|---|---|---|
| Loa | Lht | Et | 12-14 m |
| GT | TJB | TB | 15-20 |
| hp | ch | cv | 50-100 |

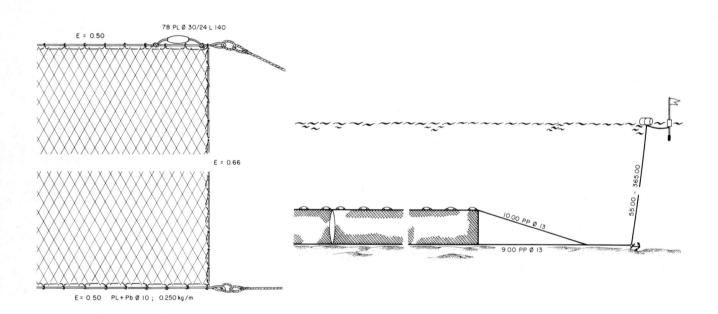

90.00 PP Ø 13

2.50 PP Ø 6   150   150 mm   1200   1200   PA MONO Ø 0.75   150   2.50 PP Ø 6

90.00 PP Ø 10

0 2 4 6 8 10    20 m

E = 0.50

78 PL Ø 30/24 L 140

E = 0.66

E = 0.50   PL + Pb Ø 10 ; 0.250 kg/m

55.00 - 365.00

10.00 PP Ø 13

9.00 PP Ø 13

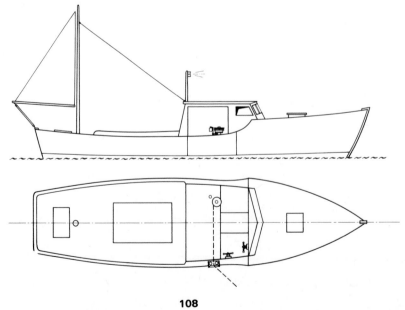

# GILLNET

Bottom set
Shark
Australia

# FILET MAILLANT

Calé sur le fond
Requin
Australie

# RED DE ENMALLE

De fondo, calada
Tiburón
Australia

### REFERENCE

W.D. Hughes
Fisheries Division
Department of Primary Industry
Canberra, Australia

| VESSEL | BATEAU | BARCO | |
|--------|--------|-------|--------|
| Loa | Lht | Et | 9-15 m |
| GT | TJB | TB | - |
| hp | ch | cv | 70-150 |

E = 0.67
550.00 PE (PP) Ø 6

4060

12    203 mm                                    PA  MONO  Ø 0.9              12    x 8 — 10

4060

564.00 PE (PP) Ø 6
E = 0.68

0  1  2  3  4  5 m

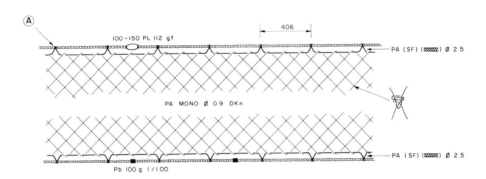

Ⓐ
100-150 PL 112 gf                406
PA (SF) (▒▒▒▒) Ø 2.5
PA MONO Ø 0.9 DKn
PA (SF) (▒▒▒▒) Ø 2.5
Pb 100 g 1/1.00

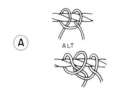

Ⓐ
ALT

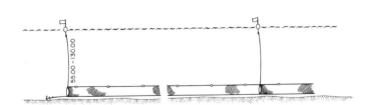

55.00 – 130.00

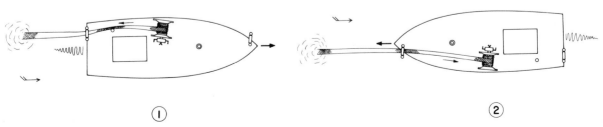

①                                              ②

**109**

# ENTANGLING NET

Bottom set
Spiny lobster
Senegal

# FILET MAILLANT

Calé sur le fond
Langouste
Sénegal

# RED DE ENMALLE

De fondo, calada
Langosta
Senegal

### REFERENCE

P. Seck
c/o Direction de l'océanographie et des pêches
Dakar, Sénegal

| VESSEL | BATEAU | BARCO | |
|--------|--------|-------|--------|
| Loa | Lht | Et | 7-12 m |
| GT | TJB | TB | - |
| hp | ch | cv | 6-20 |

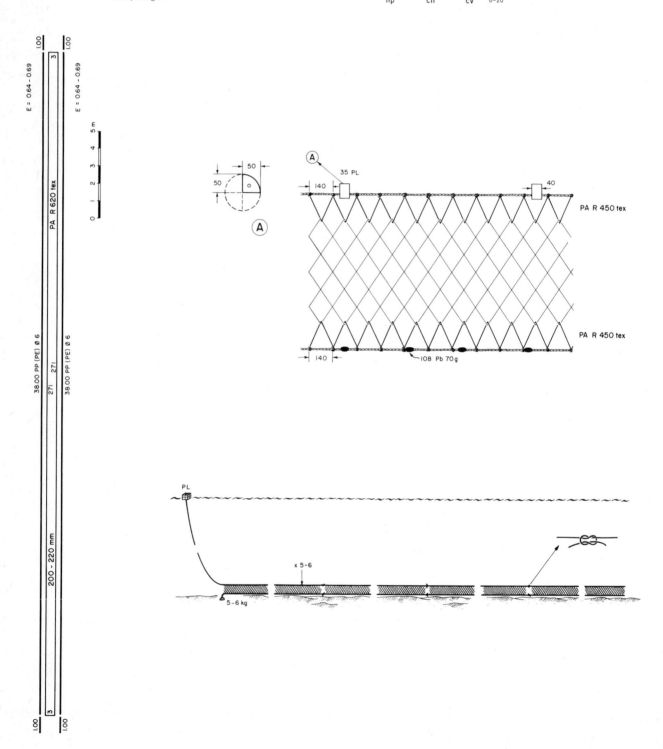

## ENTANGLING NET

Bottom set
King crab
Hokkaido, Japan

## FILET MAILLANT

Calé sur le fond
Crabe royal
Hokkaido, Japon

## RED DE ENMALLE

De fondo, calada
Cangrejo ruso
Hokkaido, Japón

REFERENCE

J. Saito

A. v. Brandt
Karlestrasse, 32
2 Hamburg 76, Fed. Rep. of Germany

VESSEL  BATEAU  BARCO

| Loa | Lht | Et | 8-9 m |
|-----|-----|-----|-------|
| GT | TJB | TB | 5-8 |
| hp | ch | cv | 46-63 |

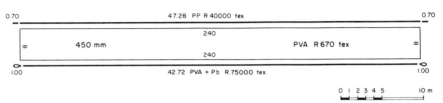

0.70      47.28 PP R 40000 tex      0.70

240

∞    450 mm      PVA R 670 tex    ∞

240

1.00      42.72 PVA + Pb R 75000 tex      1.00

0 1 2 3 4 5     10 m

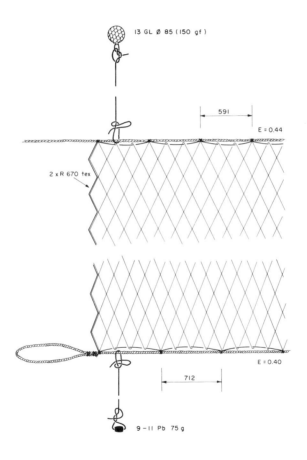

13 GL Ø 85 (150 gf)

591

E = 0.44

2 x R 670 tex

E = 0.40

712

9 - 11 Pb 75 g

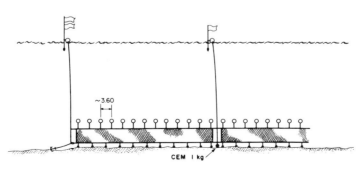

~3.60

CEM 1 kg

**111**

# ENTANGLING NET

Bottom set
Spider crab
Brittany, France

# FILET MAILLANT

Calé sur le fond
Araignée
Bretagne, France

# RED DE ENMALLE

De fondo, calada
Centolla
Bretaña, Francia

### REFERENCE

G. De Kergariou
Institut des Pêches Maritimes
Roscoff, France

| VESSEL | BATEAU | BARCO | |
|--------|--------|-------|---------|
| Loa | Lht | Et | 5-15 m |
| GT | TJB | TB | - |
| hp | ch | cv | 15-120 |

50.00 PP/PA Ø 6

| $5\frac{1}{2}$ | 320 mm | 313 / 313 | PA R 1666 tex | $5\frac{1}{2}$ |

50.00 PP/PA Ø 6

0 1 2 3 4 5     10 m

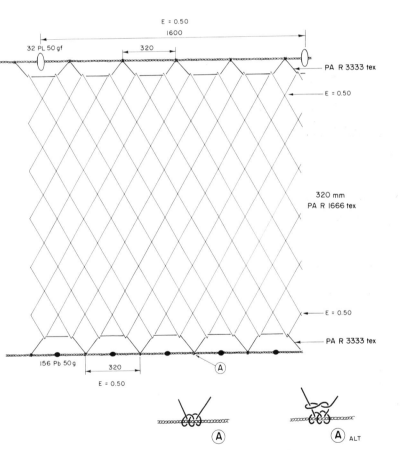

E = 0.50
1600
32 PL 50 gf
320
PA R 3333 tex
E = 0.50
320 mm
PA R 1666 tex
E = 0.50
PA R 3333 tex
156 Pb 50 g
320
(A)
E = 0.50

(A)     (A) ALT

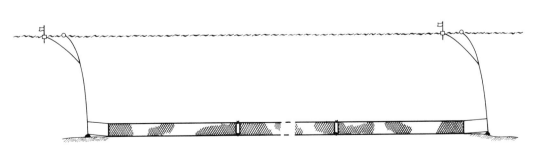

# GILLNET

Frame net, bottom set
Carp, catfish
Freshwater reservoirs
India

# FILET MAILLANT

Filet entrecroisé, calé sur le fond
Carpe, poissons chats
Lacs de barrage
Inde

# RED DE ENMALLE

Entramada, de fondo, calada
Carpa, siluros
Estanques
India

## REFERENCE

I.  V.C. George
    Institute of Fisheries, Technology Unit
    Madras, India

    A. v. Brandt, Hamburg

II. Y. Znamensky
    FAO

## VESSEL BATEAU BARCO

| | | | |
|---|---|---|---|
| Loa | Lht | Et | 5 m |
| GT | TJB | TB | - |
| hp | ch | cv | - |

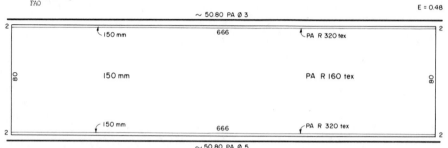

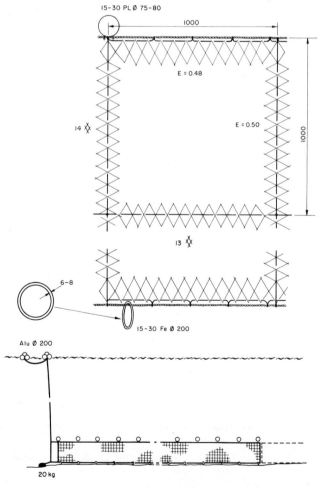

**114**

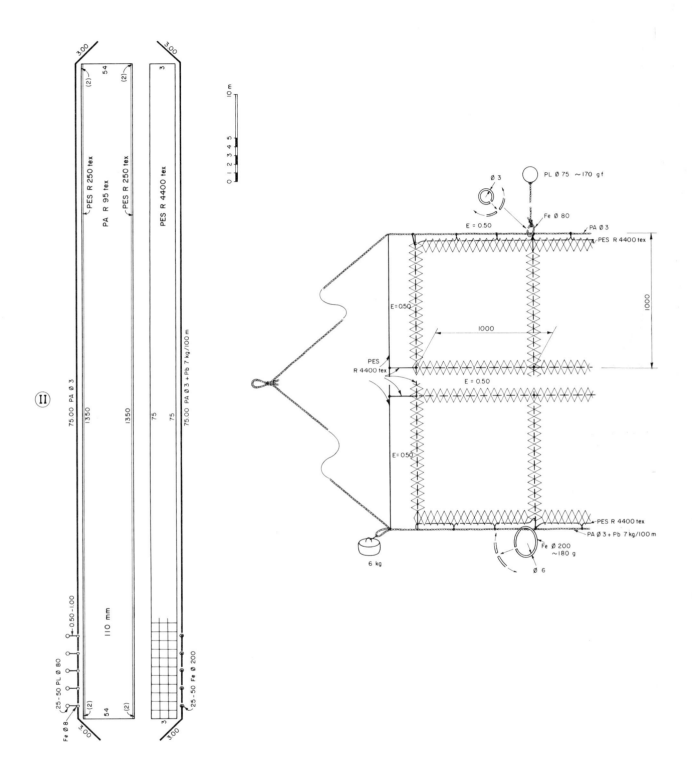

115

# ENTANGLING NET

Trammel, bottom set
Sole
E. English Channel
France

### FILET MAILLANT

Trémail, calé sur le fond
Sole
Manche E.
France

### RED DE ENMALLE

Trasmallo, de fondo, calada
Lenguado
Canal de la Mancha E.
Francia

## REFERENCE

P. Evrard
COPEBO, Boulogne-sur-Mer, France

J.C. Brabant, L. Libert
Institut des Pêches Maritimes
Boulogne-sur-Mer, France

| VESSEL | BATEAU | BARCO | |
|--------|--------|-------|--------|
| Loa | Lht | Et | 7-9 m |
| GT | TJB | TB | 6-8 |
| hp | ch | cv | 40-75 |

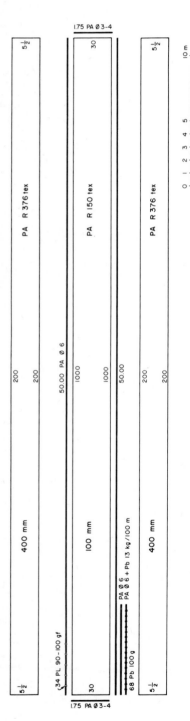

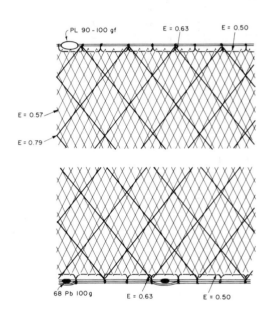

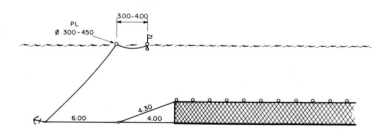

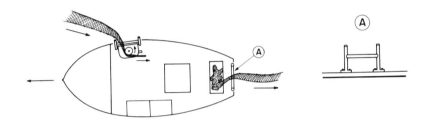

# ENTANGLING NET

Trammel, bottom set
Sole
Mediterranean, France

# FILET MAILLANT

Trémail, calé sur le fond
Sole
Méditerranée, France

# RED DE ENMALLE

Trasmallo, de fondo, calada
Lenguado
Mediterráneo, Francia

## REFERENCE

M. Bonnet
Institut des Pêches Maritimes
Nantes, France

A. Brème
FAO

## VESSEL BATEAU BARCO

| | | | |
|---|---|---|---|
| Loa | Lht | Et | 7-13 m |
| GT | TJB | TB | - |
| hp | ch | cv | 20-100 |

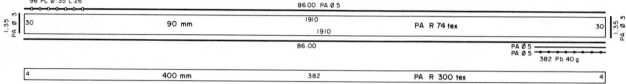

| 4 | 400 mm | 384 | PA R 300 tex | 4 |
|---|---|---|---|---|

96 PL Ø 35 L 26    86.00 PA Ø 5

| 1.35 PA Ø 3 | 30 | 90 mm | 1910 / 1910 | PA R 74 tex | 30 | 1.35 PA Ø 3 |

86.00    PA Ø 5 / PA Ø 5    382 Pb 40 g

| 4 | 400 mm | 382 | PA R 300 tex | 4 |
|---|---|---|---|---|

0 1 2 3 4 5    10 m

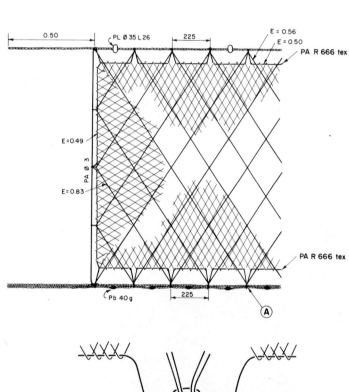

0.50    PL Ø 35 L 26    225    E = 0.56 / E = 0.50    PA R 666 tex

E = 0.49    PA Ø 3    E = 0.83

PA R 666 tex

Pb 40 g    225    (A)

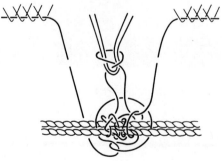

(A)

**118**

# ENTANGLING NET

Trammel, bottom set
Spiny lobster, bottom fishes
Balearic Isl., Spain

# FILET MAILLANT

Trémail, calé sur le fond
Langouste, poissons de fond
Baleares, Espagne

# RED DE ENMALLE

Trasmallo, de fondo, calada
Langosta, peces de fondo
Baleares, España

## REFERENCE

M. Massuti
Instituto Español de Oceanografía
Laboratorio de Baleares
Palma de Mallorca, Spain

| VESSEL | BATEAU | BARCO | |
|--------|--------|-------|--------|
| Loa | Lht | Et | 9-10 m |
| GT | TJB | TB | 5-6 |
| hp | ch | cv | 45-70 |

50.00 - 60.00 PP(PE) Ø 6

| 4½ | 410 mm | 200 / 200 | PA R 530 tex | 4½ |
|-----|--------|-----------|--------------|-----|
| 25 | 100 mm | 1000 / 1000 | PA R 380 tex | 25 |
| 4½ | 410 mm | 200 / 200 | PA R 530 tex | 4½ |

50.00 - 60.00 PP(PE) Ø 6

0 1 2 3 4 5    10 m

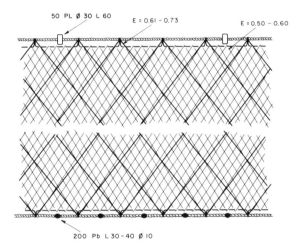

50 PL Ø 30 L 60

E = 0.61 - 0.73

E = 0.50 - 0.60

200 Pb L 30 - 40 Ø 10

# ENTANGLING NET

Combined, trammel-gillnet
Bottom set
Bottom and pelagic fishes
Mediterranean, France

# FILET MAILLANT

Combiné, Trémail-filet maillant
Calé sur le fond
Poissons de fond et pélagiques
Méditerranée, France

# RED DE ENMALLE

Combinada, trasmallo-red de enmalle
Peces de fondo y pelágicos
Mediterráneo, Francia

### REFERENCE

A. Brème
FAO

| VESSEL | BATEAU | BARCO | |
|--------|--------|-------|------|
| Loa | Lht | Et | 6-8 m |
| GT | TJB | TB | - |
| hp | ch | cv | 20-60 |

x 8-40
84.25 PA Ø 6

| 50 | 62 mm | 1720 | PA R 100 tex | 50 | (A) |
|----|-------|------|--------------|-----|-----|
| | | 2 x 96.32 | PA R 1667 tex | | |
| 3 ½ | 420 mm | 344 | PA R 300 tex | 3 ½ | (C) |
| 50 | 50 mm | 3440 | PA R 100 tex | 50 | (B) |
| 3 ½ | 420 mm | 344 | PA R 300 tex | 3 ½ | (C) |

2 x 86.00 PA (SF) Ø 6

0 1 2 3 4 5        10 m

115 PL L 30 Ø 55
245
E = 0.79
PA R 667 tex
(A)
280
E = 0.90
PA (SF) R 200 tex
E = 0.67
E = 0.56
(B)
(C) x 2
E = 0.50
PA R 667 tex
E = 0.60
430 Pb 40 g
250

ALT

Usual setting
(I) Calage habituel
Calado normal

Barrier setting
(II) Calage en barrière
Calado de barrera

# GILLNET

Driftnet
Herring
Hokkaido, Japan

# FILET MAILLANT

Dérivant
Hareng
Hokkaido, Japon

# RED DE ENMALLE

De deriva
Arenque
Hokkaido, Japón

## REFERENCE

A. v. Brandt
Karlestrasse 32
2 Hamburg 76, Fed. Rep. of Germany

| VESSEL | BATEAU | BARCO | |
|--------|--------|-------|-----------|
| Loa | Lht | Et | 12-13 m |
| GT | TJB | TB | 8-10 |
| hp | ch | cv | 50-100 |

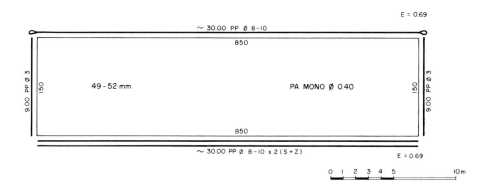

E = 0.69

~ 30.00 PP ∅ 8-10

850

9.00 PP ∅ 3    150    49 - 52 mm    PA MONO ∅ 0.40    150    9.00 PP ∅ 3

850

~ 30.00 PP ∅ 8-10 x 2 ( S + Z )

E = 0.69

0  1  2  3  4  5     10 m

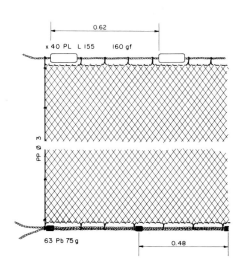

0.62

x 40 PL L 155    160 gf

PP ∅ 3

63 Pb 75 g

0.48

## GILLNET

Driftnet
Spanish mackerel
Gulf of Siam, Thailand

## FILET MAILLANT

Dérivant
Maquereau bonite
Golfe du Siam, Thaïland

## RED DE ENMALLE

De deriva
Carita
Golfo de Siam, Tailandia

### REFERENCE

A. v. Brandt
Karlestrasse 32
2 Hamburg 76, Fed. Rep. of Germany

### VESSEL  BATEAU  BARCO

| Loa | Lht | Et | 16 m |
|-----|-----|-----|------|
| GT | TJB | TB | 20 |
| hp | ch | cv | 83-175 |

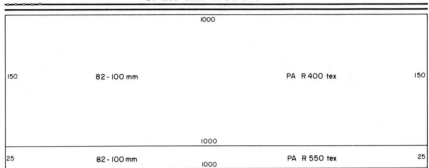

E = ~0.50

25 PL L100 Ø 50    2 x 49.00 - 50.00 PVA Ø 5  Z + S

1000

150    82 - 100 mm    PA R 400 tex    150

1000

25    82 - 100 mm    PA R 550 tex    25

1000

0 1 2 3 4 5    10 m

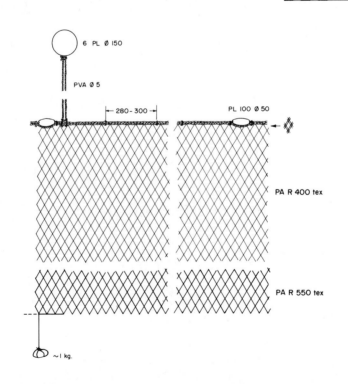

6 PL Ø 150

PVA Ø 5

280 - 300

PL 100 Ø 50

PA R 400 tex

PA R 550 tex

~1 kg.

→ 7 000 m

# GILLNET

Driftnet
Skipjack, yellowfin, bonito, shark
Sri Lanka

# FILET MAILLANT

Dérivant
Listao, albacore, bonite, requin
Sri Lanka

# RED DE ENMALLE

De deriva
Listado, rabil, bonito, tiburón
Sri Lanka

### REFERENCE

G. Pajot
FAO

### VESSEL BATEAU BARCO

| Loa | Lht | Et | – |
| GT | TJB | TB | 3.5-11 |
| hp | ch | cv | 15-70 |

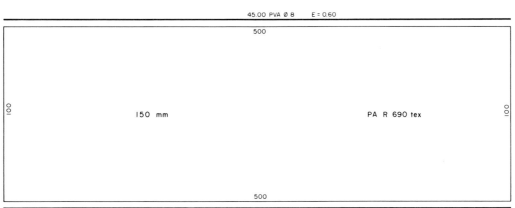

45.00 PVA Ø 8     E = 0.60

500

100

150 mm                    PA R 690 tex

100

500

45.00 PVA Ø 4     E = 0.60

0  1  2  3  4  5                    10 m

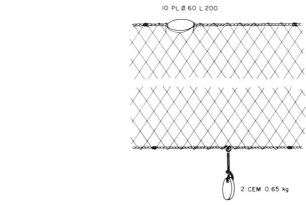

10 PL Ø 60 L 200

2 CEM 0.65 kg

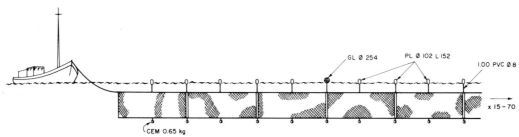

GL Ø 254     PL Ø 102 L 152     1.00 PVC Ø 8

x 15 - 70

CEM 0.65 kg

123

# GILLNET

Driftnet
Bluefin tuna
Mediterranean, France

# FILET MAILLANT

Dérivant
Thon rouge
Méditerranée, France

# RED DE ENMALLE

De deriva
Atún
Mediterráneo, Francia

## REFERENCE

P.Y. Dremière (d'après Albanez)
Institut des Pêches Maritimes
Sète, France

VESSEL  BATEAU  BARCO

| | | | |
|---|---|---|---|
| Loa | Lht | Et | 10-13 m |
| GT | TJB | TB | - |
| hp | ch | cv | 100 |

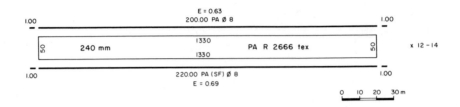

E = 0.63
1.00   200.00 PA Ø 8   1.00

| 50 | 240 mm | 1330 | PA R 2666 tex | 50 | x 12 - 14 |
| | | 1330 | | | |

1.00   220.00 PA (SF) Ø 8   1.00
E = 0.69

0   10   20   30 m

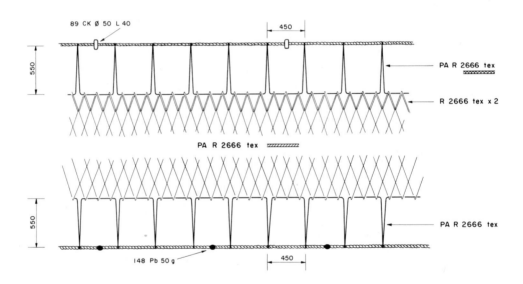

89 CK Ø 50 L 40          450

550

PA R 2666 tex

R 2666 tex x 2

PA R 2666 tex

550

PA R 2666 tex

148 Pb 50 g          450

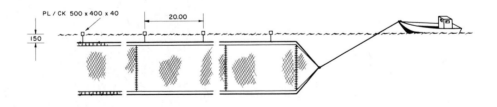

PL / CK 500 x 400 x 40          20.00

150

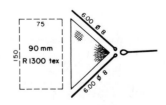

75

150   90 mm
R 1300 tex

6.00 Ø 8

6.00 Ø 8

124

# GILLNET

Driftnet
Salmon
Puget Sound, Wa., U.S.A.

# FILET MAILLANT

Dérivant
Saumon
Puget Sound, Wa., E.U.

# RED DE ENMALLE

De deriva
Salmón
Puget Sound, Wa., EE.UU.

## REFERENCE

F. Wathne
National Marine Fisheries Service
Northwest Fisheries Center
2725 Montlake Boulevard East
Seattle, Wa. 98112
U.S.A.

| VESSEL | BATEAU | BARCO | |
|--------|--------|-------|-------|
| Loa | Lht | Et | 8-12 m |
| GT | TJB | TB | - |
| hp | ch | cv | 65-320 |

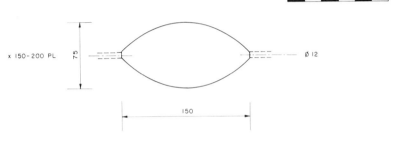

E = 0.42

150 – 200 PL    183.00 PE (PP) (PES) Ø 9.5 – 12

3140

120    138 mm    PA R 250 – 830 tex    120    x 3
(125 – 220 mm)

3140

190.00 PES + PP + Pb 38 – 54 kg / 183.00
E = 0.44

0  5  10  15  20  25  30 m

x 150 – 200 PL    75    Ø 12

150

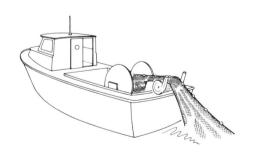

125

# GILLNET

Driftnet
Shrimp
Coastal backwater
Malabar, India

# FILET MAILLANT

Dérivant
Crevette
Bras d'eau côtiers
Malabar, Inde

# RED DE ENMALLE

De deriva
Camarón
Remansos costeros
Malabar, India

## REFERENCE

V.C. George
Institute of Fisheries, Technology Unit
Madras, India

A. v. Brandt, Hamburg, Fed. Rep. of Germany

| VESSEL | BATEAU | BARCO | |
|--------|--------|-------|------|
| Loa | Lht | Et | 5-7 m |
| GT | TJB | TB | − |
| hp | ch | cv | − |

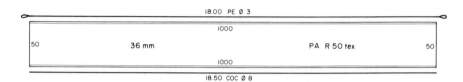

18.00 PE Ø 3

1000

50     36 mm        PA R 50 tex     50

1000

18.50 COC Ø 8

0   1   2   3   4   5 m

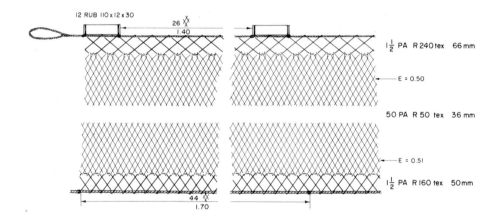

12 RUB 110 x 12 x 30

26

1.40

1½ PA R 240 tex   66 mm

E = 0.50

50 PA R 50 tex   36 mm

E = 0.51

1½ PA R 160 tex   50mm

44

1.70

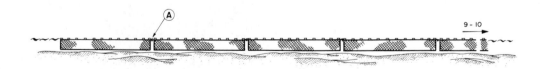

9 - 10

(A)

# GILLNET

Encircling
Sardinella
Senegal

# FILET MAILLANT

Encerclant
Sardinelle
Sénégal

# RED DE ENMALLE

De cerco
Alacha
Senegal

### REFERENCE

P. Seck
c/o Direction de l'océanographie et des pêches
Dakar, Sénégal

VESSEL BATEAU BARCO

| | | | |
|---|---|---|---|
| Loa | Lht | Et | 12 m |
| GT | TJB | TB | - |
| hp | ch | cv | 18-20 |

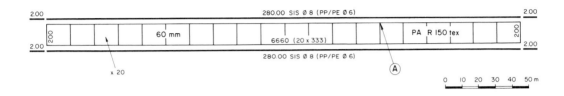

2.00      280.00 SIS Ø 8 (PP/PE Ø 6)      2.00

60 mm

6660 (20 x 333)

PA R 150 tex

2.00      280.00 SIS Ø 8 (PP/PE Ø 6)      2.00

Ⓐ

x 20

0  10  20  30  40  50 m

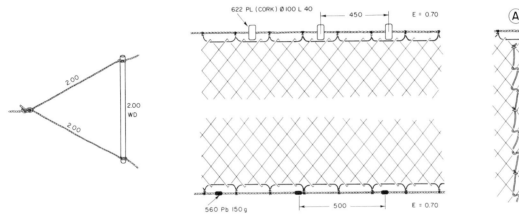

622 PL (CORK) Ø 100 L 40     450     E = 0.70

560 Pb 150 g     500     E = 0.70

2.00

2.00 WD

2.00

Ⓐ

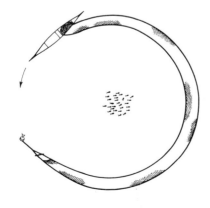

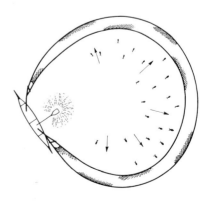

127

GILLNET

I. Driftnet
II. Surrounding
Sardine
Mediterranean, France

FILET MAILLANT

I. Dérivant
II. Encerclant
Sardine
Méditerranée, France

RED DE ENMALLE

I. De deriva
II. De cerco
Sardina
Mediterráneo, Francia

REFERENCE

P.Y. Dremière (d'après Albanez)
Institut des Pêches Maritimes
Sète, France

| VESSEL | BATEAU | BARCO | |
|--------|--------|-------|--------|
| Loa | Lht | Et | 10-13 m |
| GT | TJB | TB | - |
| hp | ch | cv | 100 |

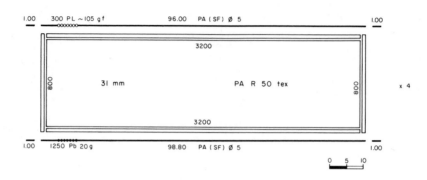

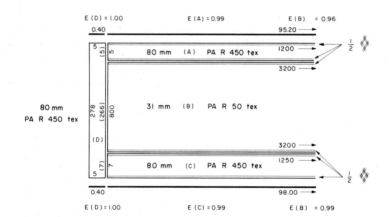

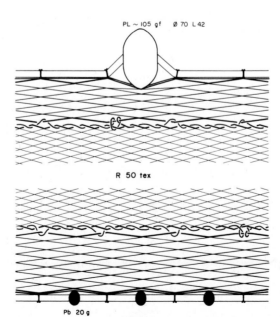

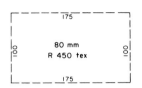

175

80 mm
R 450 tex

100                    100

175

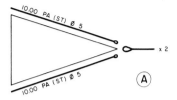

10.00  PA (ST) Ø 5

10.00  PA (ST) Ø 5

x 2

Ⓐ

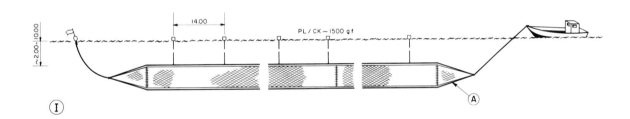

~2.00–10.00

14.00

PL / CK ~1500 gf

Ⓐ

Ⓘ

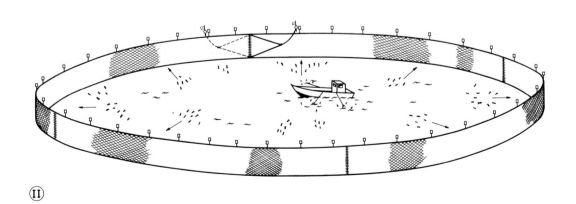

Ⓘ

# POT

Fish
Freshwater species
Lake Kossou
Ivory Coast

# NASSE

A poissons
Espèces d'eau douce
Lac de Kossou
Côte-d'Ivoire

# NASA

Para peces
Especies de agua dulce
Lago Kossou
Costa de Marfil

### REFERENCE

K.N. Niaba
c/o Autorité pour l'aménagement de la Vallée du Bandama (A.V.B.)
Côte-d'Ivoire

G.T. Taylor
FAO

| VESSEL | BATEAU | BARCO | FAC |
|--------|--------|-------|-----|
| Loa | Lht | Et | 5 m |
| GT | TJB | TB | - |
| hp | ch | cv | - |

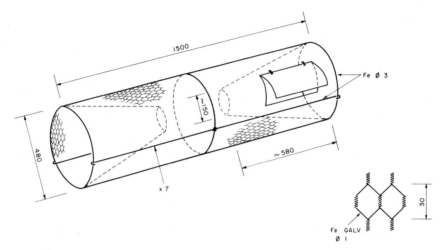

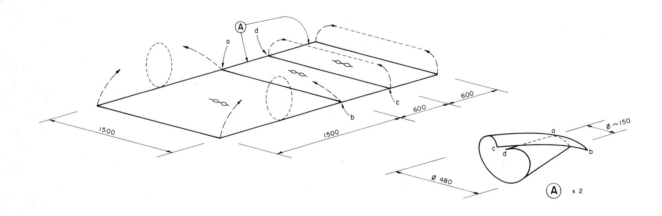

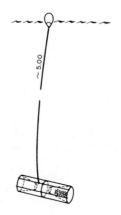

**130**

## POT

Fish
Tench, roach, carps
Lakes, rivers with slight current
Fed. Rep. of Germany

### REFERENCE

A.v. Brandt
Hamburg, Fed. Rep. of Germany

M. Kaulin
Maikammer, Fed. Rep. of Germany

## NASSE

A poissons
Tanche, gardon, carpes
Lacs, fleuves à faible courant
Rép. Féd. d'Allemagne

## NASA

Para peces
Tenca, bermejuela, carpas
Lagos, ríos con corrientes débiles
Rep. Fed. de Alemania

| VESSEL BATEAU BARCO | | | |
|---|---|---|---|
| Loa | Lht | Et | 4 – 6 m |
| GT | TJB | TB | – |
| hp | ch | cv | – |

### ALT MAT

| mm | PA R tex | MONO Ø mm |
|---|---|---|
| 24 | 150 | 0.35 |
| 36 | 230 | 0.40 |
| 72 | 380 | 0.50 |
| 80 | 455 | 0.60 |

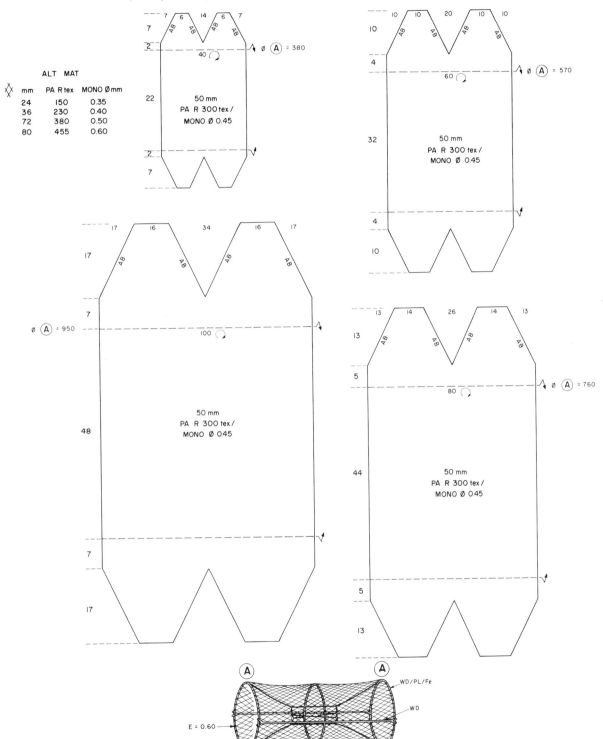

# POT

Red snapper
Spiny lobster
Venezuela

# NASSE

Vivaneau
Langouste
Venezuela

# NASA

Castañuela
Langosta
Venezuela

## REFERENCE

T. Mihara
FAO

| VESSEL | BATEAU | BARCO | |
|--------|--------|-------|------|
| Loa | Lht | Et | 10 m |
| GT | TJB | TB | - |
| hp | ch | cv | 20-30 |

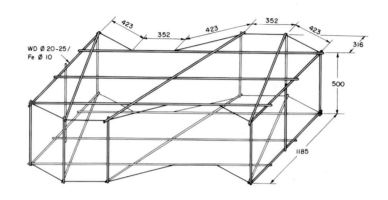

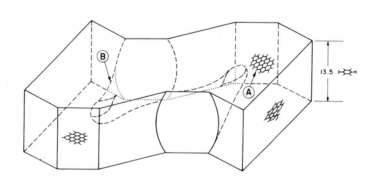

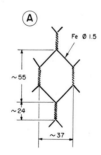

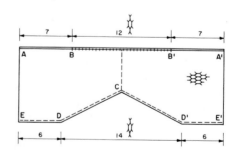

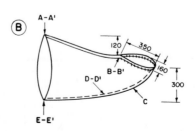

132

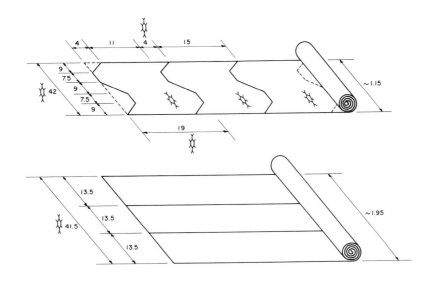

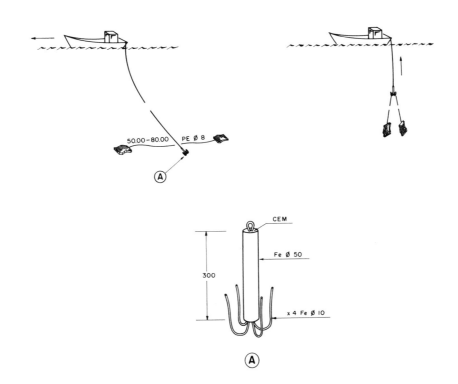

133

# POT
Crab
Hokkaido, Japan

# NASSE
Crabe
Hokkaïdo, Japon

# NASA
Cangrejo
Hokkaido, Japón

### REFERENCE
A. v. Brandt
Karlestrasse 32
2 Hamburg 76, Fed. Rep. of Germany

| VESSEL | BATEAU | BARCO | |
|--------|--------|-------|----------|
| Loa | Lht | Et | 10-14 m |
| GT | TJB | TB | 10-15 |
| hp | ch. | cv | 75-120 |

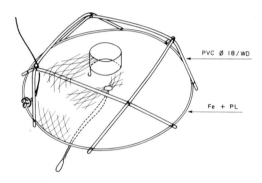

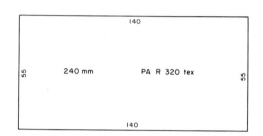

140

55    240 mm    PA R 320 tex    55

140

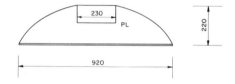

134

# POT

Crab
I. Hokkaido, Japan
II. Newfoundland, Canada

# NASSE

Crabe
I. Hokkaïdo, Japon
II. Terre-Neuve, Canada

# NASA

Cangrejo
I. Hokkaido, Japón
II. Terranova, Canadá

## REFERENCE

I. A. v. Brandt
   Hamburg, Fed. Rep. of Germany

II. A.J. Provan, R.G. Kingsley
    College of Fisheries
    St. John's, Newfoundland
    Canada

VESSEL BATEAU BARCO

| | | | |
|---|---|---|---|
| Loa | Lht | Et | 12-15 m |
| GT | TJB | TB | - |
| hp | ch | cv | 40-100 |

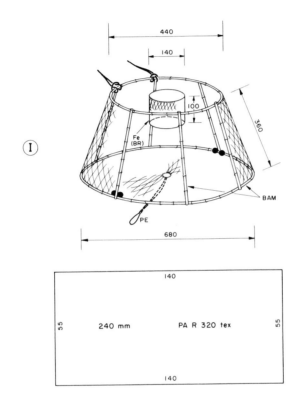

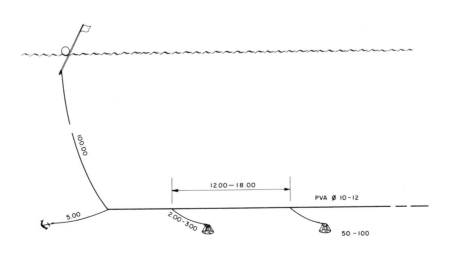

**135**

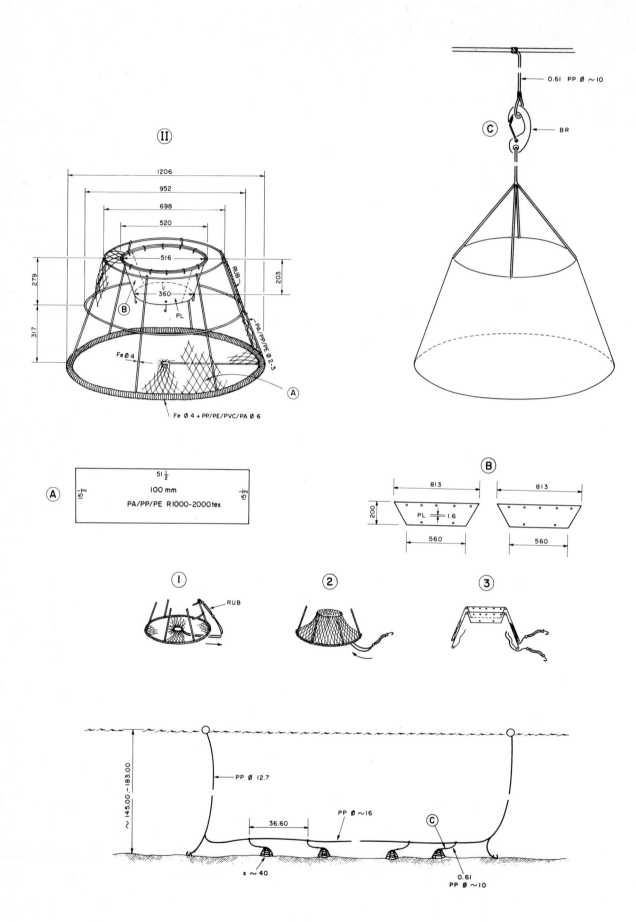

II

1206
952
698
520
516
279
317
203
360
RUB
PL
B
PA/PP/PE Ø 2-3
Fe Ø 4
A
Fe Ø 4 + PP/PE/PVC/PA Ø 6

0.61 PP Ø ~10
C
BR

A
51½
15½    100 mm    15½
PA/PP/PE R1000-2000tex

B
813                813
200
PL  1.6
560                560

1    RUB

2

3

PP Ø 12.7
~ 145.00.-183.00
36.60    PP Ø ~16
C
x ~ 40
0.61
PP Ø ~10

136

# POT

Spiny lobster
Brittany, France

# NASSE

Langouste
Bretagne, France

# NASA

Langosta
Bretaña, Francia

## REFERENCE

G. de Kergariou
Institut des pêches maritimes
Roscoff, France

## VESSEL BATEAU BARCO

| Loa | Lht | Et | 5-15 m |
|-----|-----|-----|--------|
| GT | TJB | TB | - |
| hp | ch | cv | 15-120 |

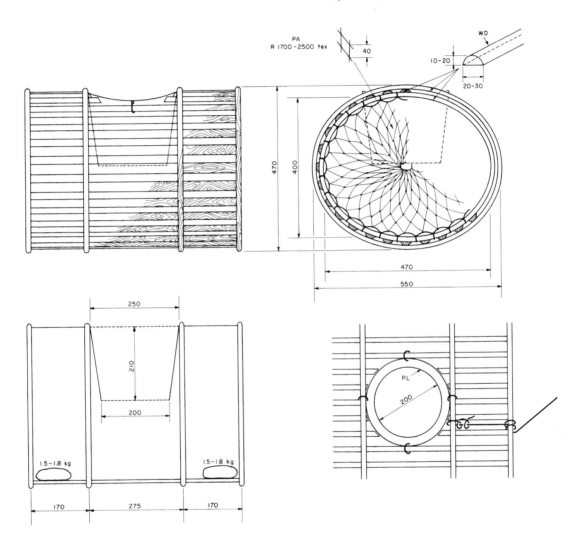

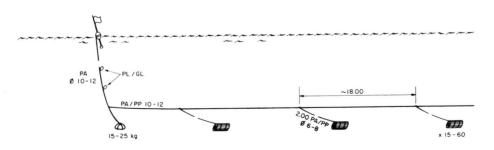

137

# POT

Norway lobster (Nephrops)
Scotland

# NASSE

Langoustine
Ecosse

# NASA

Cigala
Escocia

## REFERENCE

W. Stewart
13 Dunbar Street
Lossiemouth IV31 6AG
Morayshire, Scotland

## VESSEL BATEAU BARCO

| Loa | Lht | Et | 9 m |
|-----|-----|-----|-----|
| GT | TJB | TB | - |
| hp | ch | cv | 30 |

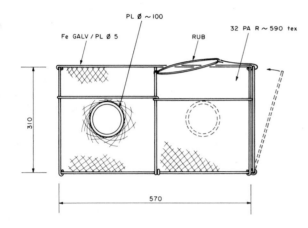

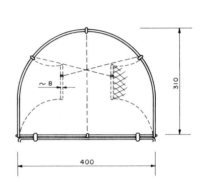

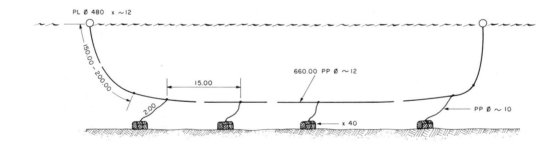

# POT

Octopus
With bait
Japan

# NASSE

Poulpe
Avec appât
Japon

# NASA

Pulpo
Con carnada
Japón

## REFERENCE

Ubara Fishermen's Association
Japan

T. Mihara
FAO

## VESSEL BATEAU BARCO

| Loa | Lht | Et | 10-15 m |
|-----|-----|-----|---------|
| GT  | TJB | TB | – |
| hp  | ch  | cv | 20-75 |

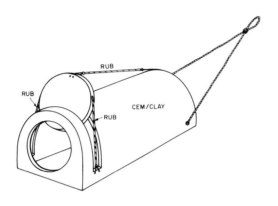

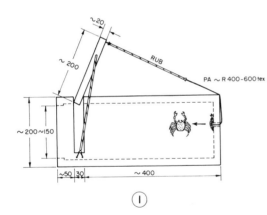

① 

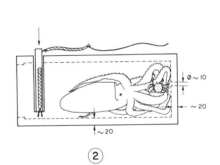

② 

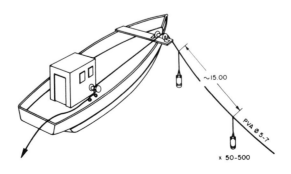

Lobster (creel)
E. Scotland

A homard
Ecosse E.

Para bogavante
Escocia E.

REFERENCE

W. Stewart
Lossiemouth, Scotland

VESSEL BATEAU BARCO

| Loa | Lht | Et | 9 – 10 m |
|-----|-----|-----|----------|
| GT | TJB | TB | – |
| hp | ch | cv | – |

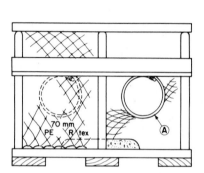

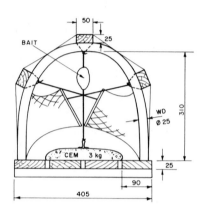

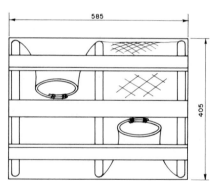

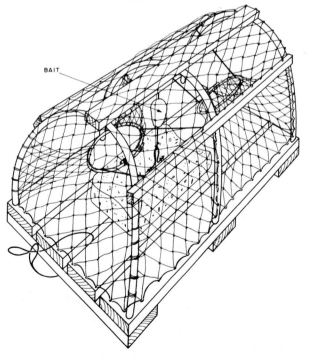

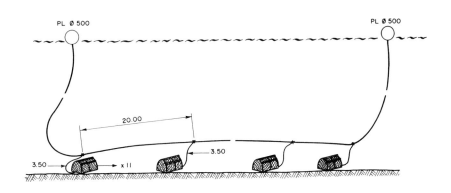

PL Ø 500          PL Ø 500

20.00

3.50

3.50          x II

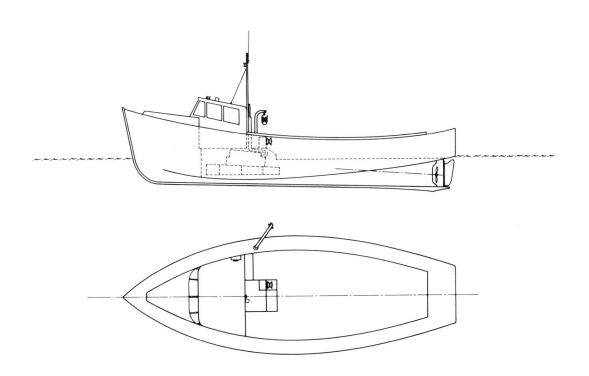

141

**POT**

Lobster
Rectangular type
Buzzards Bay (Mass.), U.S.A.

**NASSE**

A homard
Type rectangulaire
Buzzards Bay, E.U.

**NASA**

Para bogavante
Tipo rectangular
Buzzards Bay, EE.UU.

REFERENCE

J.T. Everett
National Marine Fisheries Service
Washington, D.C. 20235, U.S.A.

VESSEL BATEAU BARCO

| Loa | Lht | Et | 9 - 10 m |
|-----|-----|----|----------|
| GT  | TJB | TB | - |
| hp  | ch  | cv | 100 |

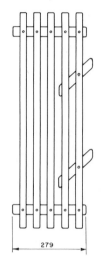

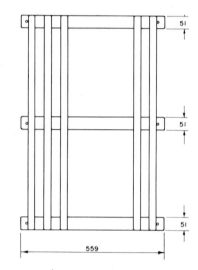

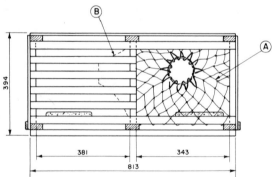

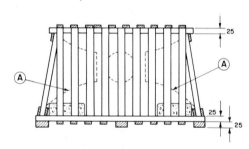

PA ~ R 2500 tex
~76 mm

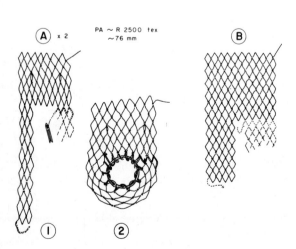

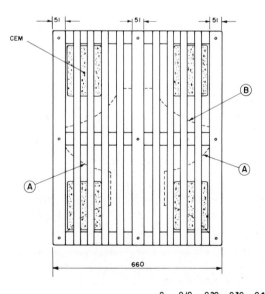

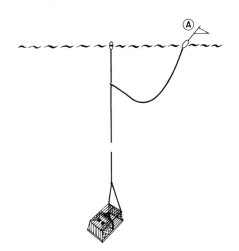

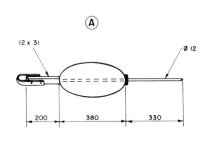

A

12 x 31

Ø 12

200    380    330

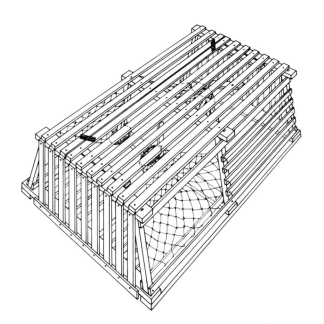

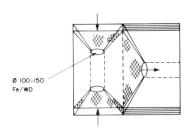

Ø 100-150
Fe/WD

# POT

Octopus
Without bait
I. Japan (Hokkaido)
II. Venezuela

## NASSE

Poulpe
Sans appât
I. Japon (Hokkaïdo)
II. Venezuela

## NASA

Pulpo
Sin carnada
I. Japón (Hokkaido)
II. Venezuela

### REFERENCE

I. A. v. Brandt
   Hamburg, Fed. Rep. of Germany

II. T. Mihara
    FAO

VESSEL BATEAU BARCO

| Loa | Lht | Et | 6-11 m |
|-----|-----|-----|--------|
| GT  | TJB | TB  | -      |
| hp  | ch  | cv  | 10-35  |

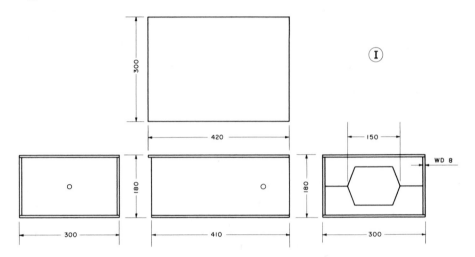

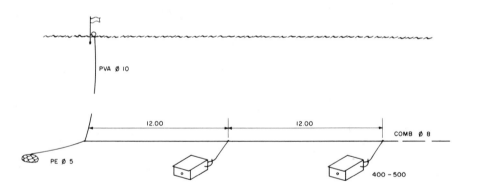

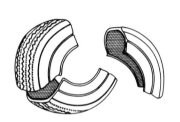

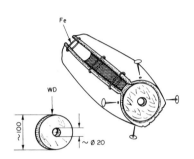

Fe

WD

~100

~ Ø 20

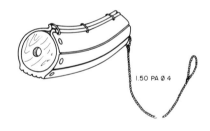

1.50 PA Ø 4

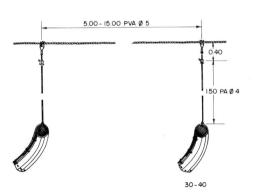

5.00 - 15.00 PVA Ø 5

0.40

1.50 PA Ø 4

30 - 40

# FYKE NET

Without wings
Eel
Rivers, Fed. Rep. of Germany

## REFERENCE

A.v. Brandt
Hamburg, Fed. Rep. of Germany

M. Kaulin
Maikammer, Fed. Rep. of Germany

# VERVEUX

Sans ailes
Anguille
Rivières, Rép. Féd. d'Allemagne

# GARLITO

Sin bandas
Anguila
Ríos, Rep. Fed. de Alemania

| VESSEL BATEAU BARCO | | | FAC |
|---|---|---|---|
| Loa | Lht | Et | 4 – 6 m |
| GT | TJB | TB | – |
| hp | ch | cv | – |

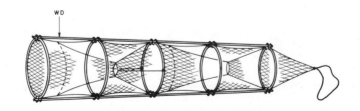

WD

146

# FYKE NET

With unequal wings
Eel, mullet
Coastal and lagoon waters
Adriatic, Italy

### REFERENCE

G. Bombace, N. Frontini, B. Antolini
Laboratorio di Tecnologia della pesca
Ancona, Italy

# VERVEUX

A ailes inégales
Anguille, mulet
Eaux côtières et lagunaires
Adriatique, Italie

# GARLITO

Con bandas desiguales
Anguila, mujol
Aguas costeras y lagunares
Adriático, Italia

| VESSEL | BATEAU | BARCO | FAC |
|--------|--------|-------|-----|
| Loa | Lht | Et | – |
| GT | TJB | TB | – |
| hp | ch | cv | – |

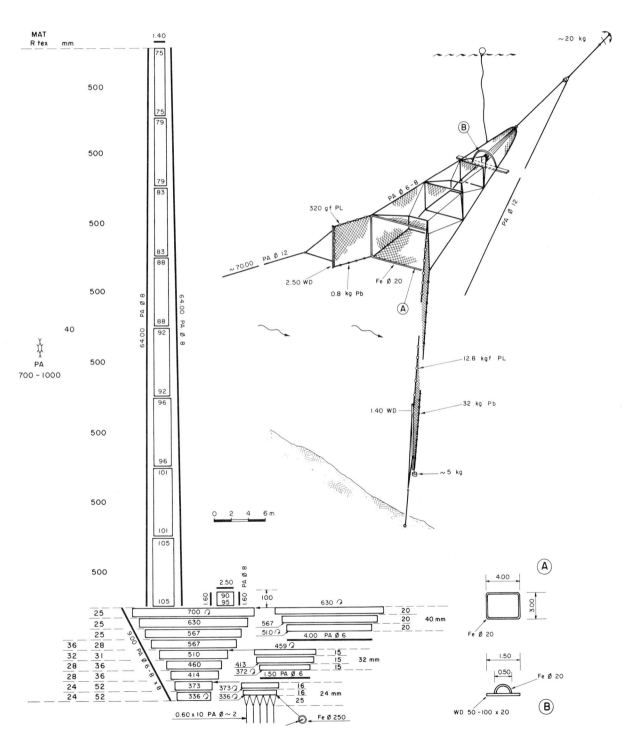

147

# FYKE NET

With leader
 I Double, moored
II Single, on stakes
Freshwater fishes
Lakes, Fed. Rep. of Germany

### REFERENCE

M. Kaulin
Maikammer, Fed. Rep. of Germany

# VERVEUX

Avec barrière
 I Double, mouillé
II Simple, sur pieux
Poissons d'eau douce
Lacs, Rép. Féd. d'Allemagne

# GARLITO

Con barrera
 I Doble, anclado
II Sencillo, con estacas
Peces de agua dulce
Lagos, Rep. Fed. de Alemania

| VESSEL | BATEAU | BARCO | |
|---|---|---|---|
| Loa | Lht | Et | 4 – 6 m |
| GT | TJB | TB | – |
| hp | ch | cv | – |

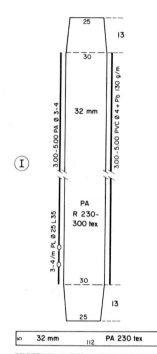

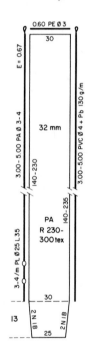

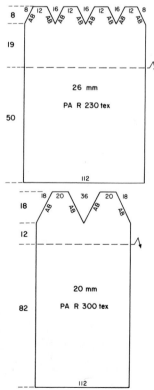

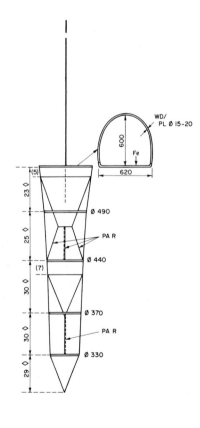

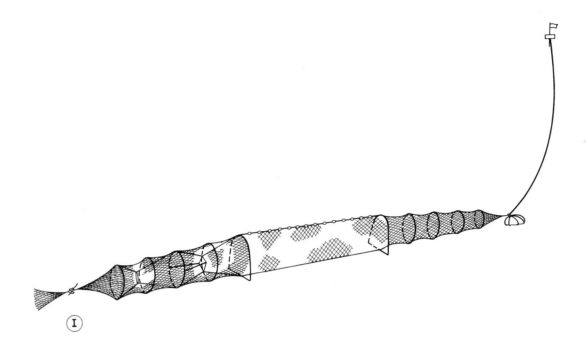

I

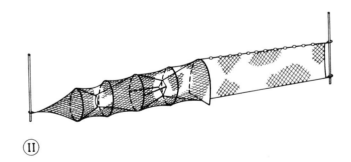

II

149

# FYKE NET

With leader and wings, triple
On stakes
Eel, sea-bream, mullet, bass
Lagoons, Mediterranean, France

### REFERENCE

P.Y. Dremière (d'après A. Hyrailles)
Institut des Pêches Maritimes
Sète, France

# VERVEUX

Avec barrière et ailes, triple
Sur pieux
Anguille, dorade, mulet, bar
Lagunes, Méditerranée, France

### VESSEL BATEAU BARCO

| Loa | Lht | Et | 4 – 6 m |
|-----|-----|-----|---------|
| GT | TJB | TB | – |
| hp | ch | cv | – |

# GARLITO

Con barrera y bandas, triple
Sobre estacas
Anguila, espáridos, mujol, lubina
Lagunas, Mediterráneo, Francia

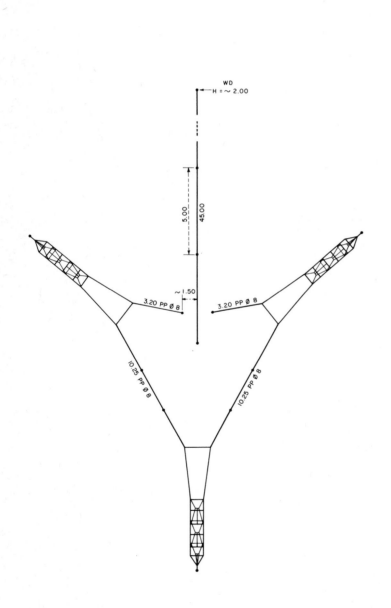

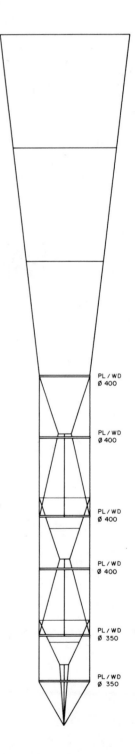

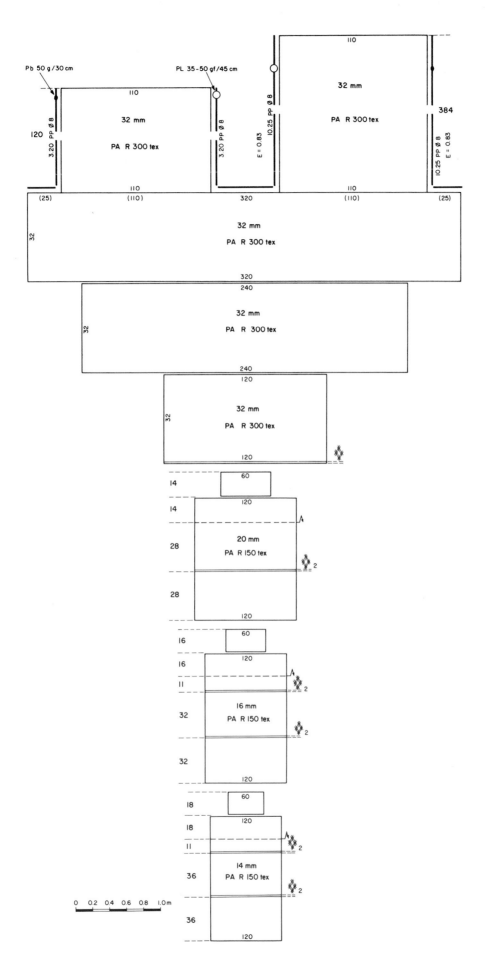

# STOWNET

Anchored
Shrimp
Lagoons, Senegal

# CHALUT A L'ETALAGE

Au mouillage
Crevette
Lagunes, Sénégal

# BITURON

Anclado
Camarón
Lagunas, Senegal

### REFERENCE

P. Seck
c/o Direction de l'océanographie et des pêches
Dakar, Sénégal

| VESSEL | BATEAU | BARCO | |
|--------|--------|-------|--------|
| Loa | Lht | Et | 5 - 6 m |
| GT | TJB | TB | - |
| hp | ch | cv | - |

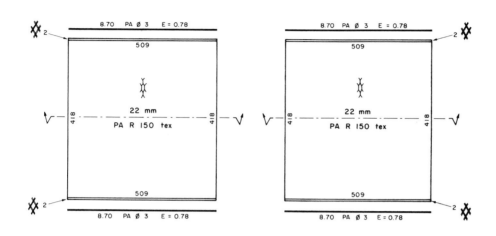

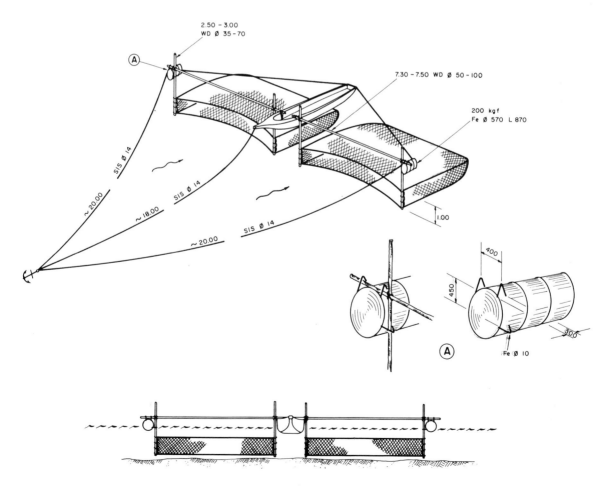

153

## VERANDA NET

Encircling
Mullet
Lagoons and coastal waters
Mediterranean, France

## CANNASSE

Encerclant
Mulet
Lagunes et eaux côtières
Méditerranée, France

## SALTADA

De cerco
Mujol
Lagunas y aguas costeras
Mediterráneo, Francia

### REFERENCE

P.Y. Dremière, J. Capelle (d'après A. Hyrailles)
Institut des Pêches Maritimes
Sète, France

| VESSEL | BATEAU | BARCO | x 2 - 3 |
|--------|--------|-------|---------|
| Loa | Lht | Et | 4 - 5 m |
| GT | TJB | TB | - |
| hp | ch | cv | - |

x 6

| 5 | 400 mm | 200 | PA R 333 tex | 5 |
|---|--------|-----|--------------|---|
| | | 200 | | |

| 0.50 | | 36.00 | PA (SF) Ø 6 | 0.50 |

| 84 | 40 mm | 1400 | PA R 100 tex | 84 |
|----|-------|------|--------------|----|
| | | 1400 | | |

| 0.50 | 100 PL 70 g f | 36.00 | PA (SF) Ø 6 | 0.50 |

| 5 | 400 mm | 200 | PA R 333 tex | 5 |
|---|--------|-----|--------------|---|
| | | 200 | | |

| 100 | 50 mm | 1000 | PA R 225 tex | 100 |
|-----|-------|------|--------------|-----|
| | | 1000 | | |

| 0.50 | 200 Pb 40 - 50 g | 36.00 | PA (SF) Ø 6 | 0.50 |

0  2  4  6  8 m

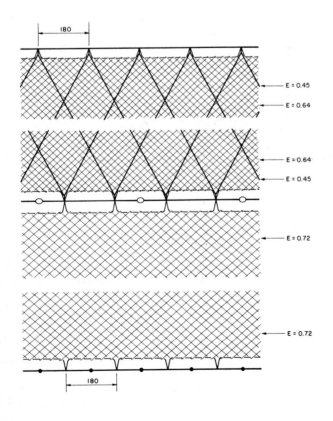

E = 0.45
E = 0.64
E = 0.64
E = 0.45
E = 0.72
E = 0.72

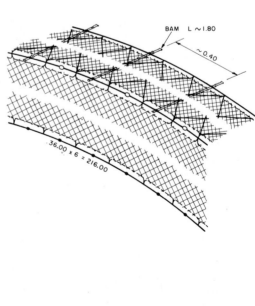

BAM L ~ 1.80
~ 0.40
36.00 x 6 = 216.00

154

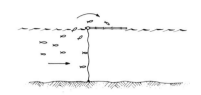

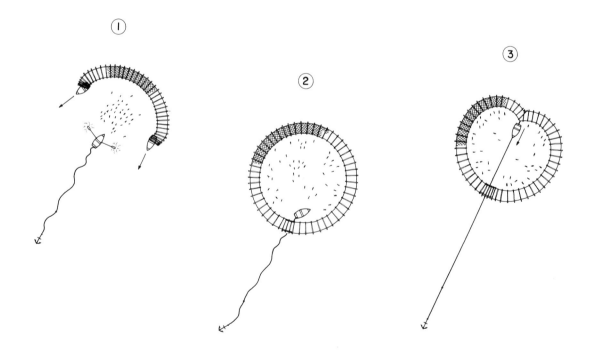

# LINES

Hand
 I Wreck bass
II Rockfish
Balearic Isl., Spain

### REFERENCE

M. Massuti
Instituto Español de Oceanografía
Laboratorio de Baleares
Palma de Mallorca, Spain

# LIGNES

A main
 I Cernier
II Rascasse
Baléares, Espagne

# LINEAS

De mano
 I Cherna
II Gallineta
Baleares, España

| VESSEL | BATEAU | BARCO | |
|--------|--------|-------|---------|
| Loa | Lht | Et | 6 - 8 m |
| GT | TJB | TB | - |
| hp | ch | cv | 20 - 50 |

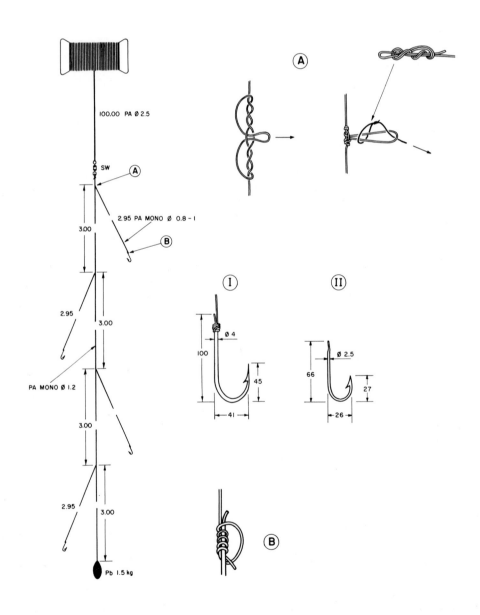

100.00 PA Ø 2.5

SW  (A)

3.00

2.95 PA MONO Ø 0.8 - 1

(B)

2.95

3.00

PA MONO Ø 1.2

3.00

2.95   3.00

Pb 1.5 kg

(A)

(I)    (II)

Ø 4

100

45

41

Ø 2.5

66

27

26

(B)

**156**

# LINES

Hand
Couch's sea bream
Venezuela

### REFERENCE

T. Mihara
FAO

# LIGNES

A main
Pagre
Venezuela

# LINEAS

De mano
Pargo
Venezuela

| VESSEL | BATEAU | BARCO | |
|--------|--------|-------|---------|
| Loa | Lht | Et | 10 - 15 m |
| GT | TJB | TB | - |
| hp | ch | cv | 30 - 90 |

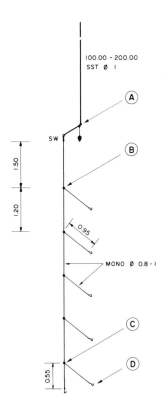

100.00 - 200.00
SST Ø 1

Ⓐ

SW

Ⓑ

1.50

1.20

0.95

MONO Ø 0.8-1

Ⓒ

Ⓓ

0.55

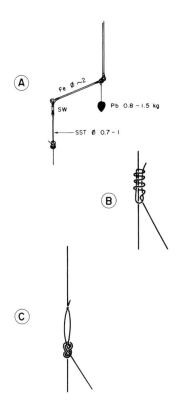

Ⓐ   Fe Ø ~2   Pb 0.8 - 1.5 kg

SW

SST Ø 0.7 - 1

Ⓑ

Ⓒ

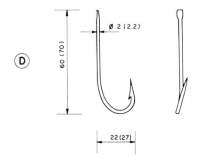

Ⓓ   Ø 2 (2.2)

60 (70)

22 (27)

# LINES

Hand, with bait pouch
Snapper, yellowtail
Japan

# LIGNES

A main, avec poche d'appât
Vivaneau, sériole
Japon

# LINEAS

De mano, con bolsillo de cebo
Castañuela, serviola
Japón

### REFERENCE

Ubara Fishermen's Association
Chiba, Japan

T. Mihara
FAO

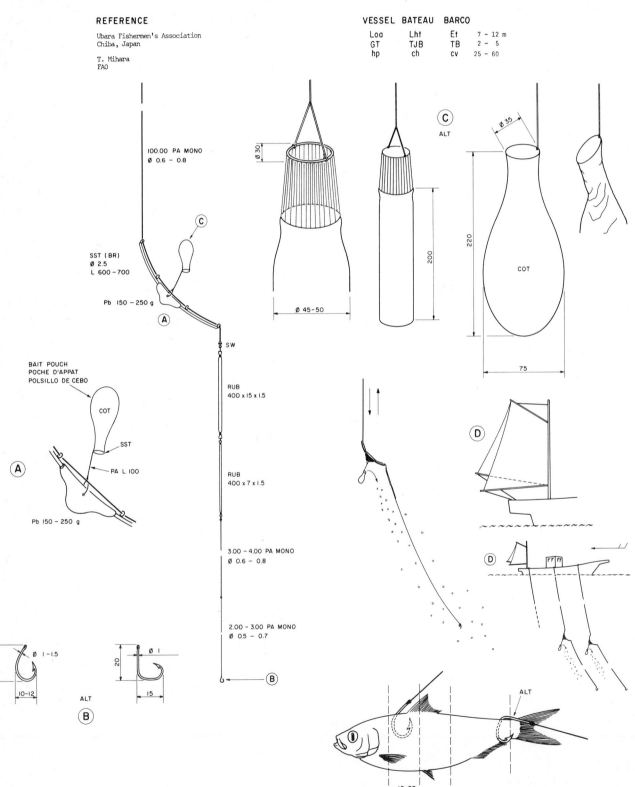

| VESSEL | BATEAU | BARCO | |
|--------|--------|-------|-----------|
| Loa | Lht | Et | 7 - 12 m |
| GT | TJB | TB | 2 - 5 |
| hp | ch | cv | 25 - 60 |

100.00 PA MONO
Ø 0.6 - 0.8

C

SST (BR)
Ø 2.5
L 600 - 700

Pb 150 - 250 g

A

SW

RUB
400 x 15 x 1.5

BAIT POUCH
POCHE D'APPAT
POLSILLO DE CEBO

COT

SST

A

PA L 100

RUB
400 x 7 x 1.5

Pb 150 - 250 g

3.00 - 4.00 PA MONO
Ø 0.6 - 0.8

2.00 - 3.00 PA MONO
Ø 0.5 - 0.7

B

Ø 30

Ø 45-50

200

C
ALT

Ø 35

220

COT

75

D

D

ALT

18 - 20

Ø 1 - 1.5

10 - 12

B
ALT

20

Ø 1

15

~ 10 - 20

158

# LINES

Hand
Yellowfin, bigeye tuna
Bashi Channel (Luzon Strait)
Taiwan, China

### REFERENCE

A.v. Brandt
Hamburg, Fed. Rep. of Germany

# LIGNES

A main
Albacore, patudo
Canal de Bashi (Dét. de Luzon)
Taiwan, Chine

# LINEAS

De mano
Rabil, patudo
Canal de Bashi (Estrecho de Luzón)
Taiwán, China

| VESSEL | BATEAU | BARCO | |
|--------|--------|-------|------|
| Loa | Lht | Et | 9 m |
| GT | TJB | TB | 5 |
| hp | ch | cv | 22 – 30 |

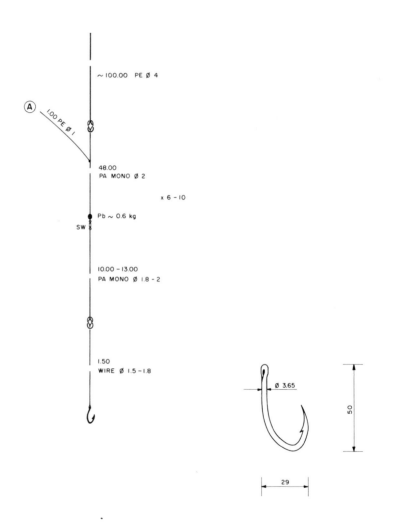

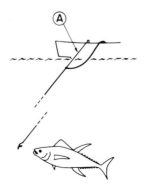

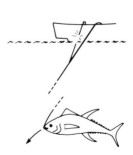

**159**

# LINES

Hand
King mackerel, Spanish mackerel
Venezuela

# LIGNES

A main
Thazard, maquereau espagnol
Venezuela

# LINEAS

De mano
Carita, estornino
Venezuela

## REFERENCE

T. Mihara
FAO

| VESSEL | BATEAU | BARCO | |
|--------|--------|-------|--------|
| Loa | Lht | Et | 8 - 10 m |
| GT | TJB | TB | - |
| hp | ch | cv | 20 - 35 |

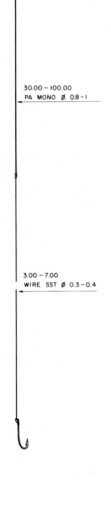

30.00 - 100.00
PA MONO Ø 0.8 - 1

3.00 - 7.00
WIRE SST Ø 0.3 - 0.4

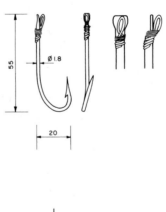

55

Ø 1.8

20

## REFERENCE

M. Sevellec
Douarnenez, France

A. Ragot
Loudéac, France

## VESSEL BATEAU BARCO

| Loa | Lht | Et | 6 - 12 m |
|-----|-----|-----|----------|
| GT | TJB | TB | - |
| hp | ch | cv | 20 - 80 |

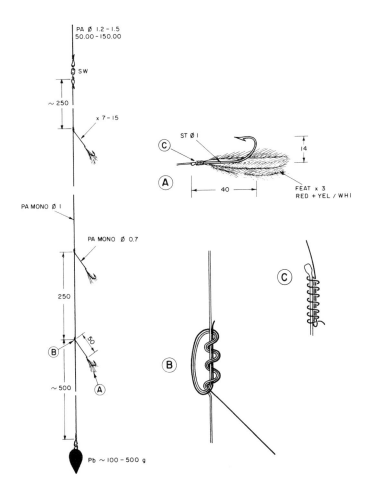

PA Ø 1.2 - 1.5
50.00 - 150.00

SW

~ 250

x 7 - 15

PA MONO Ø 1

PA MONO Ø 0.7

250

B

~ 500    A

Pb ~ 100 - 500 g

ST Ø 1

C

A

14

40

FEAT x 3
RED + YEL / WHI

C

B

# LINES

Hand, with artificial lures
Mackerel, horse mackerel
Venezuela

# LIGNES

A main, avec leurres artificiels
Maquereau, chinchard
Venezuela

# LINEAS

De mano, "ciempiés"
Caballa, chicharro
Venezuela

### REFERENCE

T. Mihara
FAO

### VESSEL BATEAU BARCO

| | | | |
|---|---|---|---|
| Loa | Lht | Et | 8 - 10 m |
| GT | TJB | TB | - |
| hp | ch | cv | 15 - 20 |

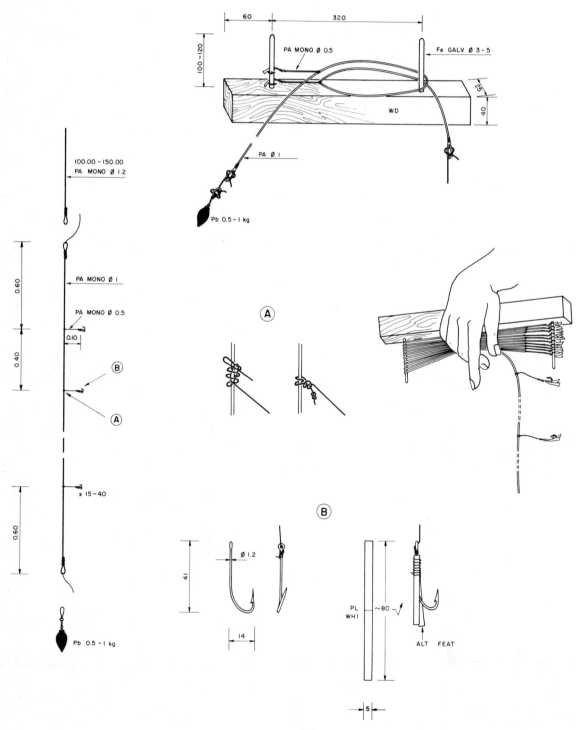

162

# LINES

Hand
Cod
Saint-Pierre and Miquelon, North-West Atlantic

# LIGNES

A main
Morue
Saint-Pierre et Miquelon, Atlantique Nord-Ouest

# LINEAS

De mano
Bacalao
Saint-Pierre y Miquelón,
Atlántico Noroeste

### REFERENCE

B. Paturel
Institut des Pêches Maritimes
Saint-Pierre et Miquelon, Amérique du Nord

### VESSEL BATEAU BARCO

| Loa | Lht | Et | 8 m |
|-----|-----|-----|--------|
| GT | TJB | TB | - |
| hp | ch | cv | 15 - 25 |

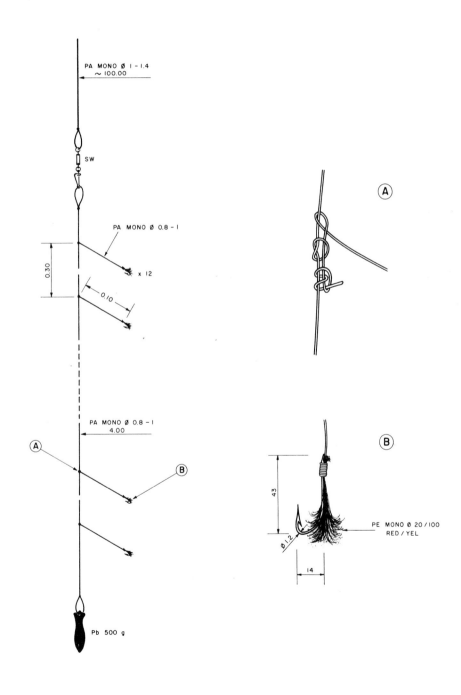

PA MONO Ø 1 - 1.4
~ 100.00

SW

PA MONO Ø 0.8 - 1

x 12

0.30

0.10

PA MONO Ø 0.8 - 1
4.00

Ⓐ

Ⓑ

Ⓐ

Ⓑ

43

Ø 1.2

14

PE MONO Ø 20 / 100
RED / YEL

Pb 500 g

## LINES

Hand, jig
Cod
Saint-Pierre and Miquelon,
North-West Atlantic

### REFERENCE

B. Paturel
Institut des Pêches Maritimes
Saint-Pierre et Miquelon
Amérique du Nord

J. Ancellin
Cherbourg, France

## LIGNES

A main, "faux", "vette"
Morue
Saint-Pierre et Miquelon,
Atlantique Nord-Ouest

## LINEAS

De mano, con anzuelo emplomado
Bacalao
Saint-Pierre y Miquelón,
Atlántico Noroeste

| VESSEL | BATEAU | BARCO | |
|---|---|---|---|
| Loa | Lht | Et | 8 m |
| GT | TJB | TB | – |
| hp | ch | cv | 15 – 25 |

PA MONO Ø 1.4
~100.00

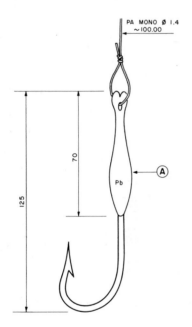

Pb

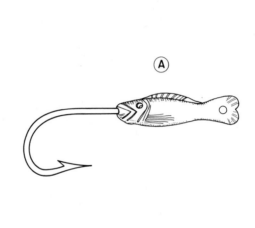

Ⓐ

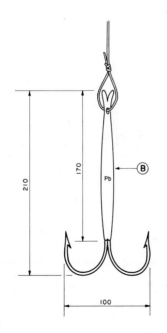

Pb

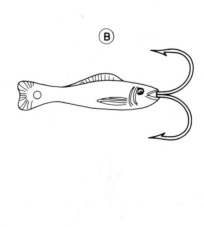

Ⓑ

# LINES

Hand, deep sea, with reel
Snapper, grouper
 I Japan
 II Fiji Islands

# LIGNES

A main, en eau profonde, avec moulinet
Vivaneau, mérou
 I Japon
 II Iles Fidji

# LINEAS

De mano, en agua profunda
 con carretel
Castañuela, cherna
 I Japón
 II Islas Fiji

## REFERENCE

I Tamehiko Uchida, Masaru Kuroki
 Miyazaki Fisheries Experimental Institute
 ("Handline fishing", Koseisha-Koseikaku, Tokyo, Japan)
 T. Mihara
 FAO

II L. Devambez
 FAO

| VESSEL | BATEAU | BARCO | |
|--------|--------|-------|--------|
| Loa | Lht | Et | 6 - 12 |
| GT | TJB | TB | 2 - 5 |
| hp | ch | cv | 10 - 45 |

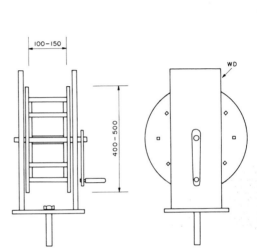

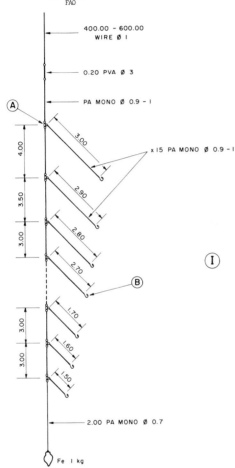

400.00 - 600.00 WIRE Ø 1

0.20 PVA Ø 3

PA MONO Ø 0.9 - 1

Ⓐ

4.00

3.00

x15 PA MONO Ø 0.9 - 1

3.50

2.90

3.00

2.80

2.70

Ⓑ

3.00

1.70

1.60

3.00

1.50

2.00 PA MONO Ø 0.7

Fe 1 kg

Ⓘ

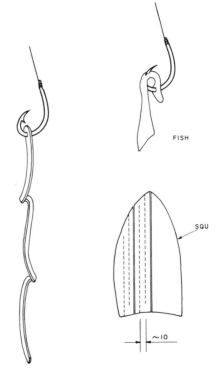

FISH

SQU

~10

WD

100-150

400-500

Ⓐ

Ø 2-3

35-45

Ⓑ

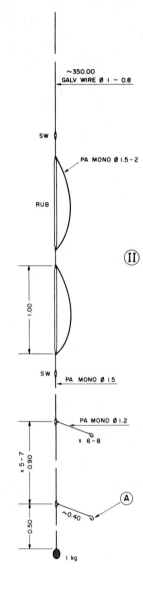

~350.00
GALV WIRE Ø 1 − 0.8

SW

PA MONO Ø 1.5 − 2

RUB

(II)

1.00

SW    PA MONO Ø 1.5

PA MONO Ø 1.2
x 6 − 8

x 5 − 7    0.90

~0.40    (A)

0.50

1 kg

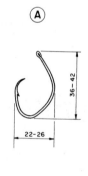

(A)

36 − 42

22 − 26

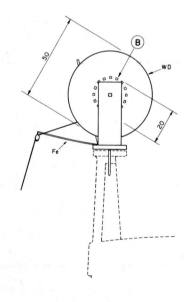

50

(B)

WD

20

Fe

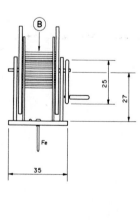

(B)

25

27

Fe

35

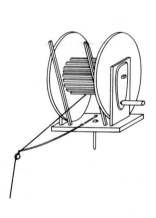

20

(B)

# LINES

Hand
With electric reel
Cod
Iceland

### REFERENCE

- Gudni Thorsteinsson
  Hafrannsóknastofnunin
  Reykjavik, Iceland

- Elektra Fishing Reel
  Ellidi Norddahl Gudjónsson
  Gardahreppur, Iceland

- G. Jonasson
  FAO

# LIGNES

A main
Avec moulinet électrique
Morue
Islande

# LINEAS

De mano
Con carretel eléctrico
Bacalao
Islandia

| VESSEL | BATEAU | BARCO | |
|--------|--------|-------|-----------|
| Loa | Lht | Et | 10 - 12 m |
| GT | TJB | TB | - |
| hp | ch | cv | - |

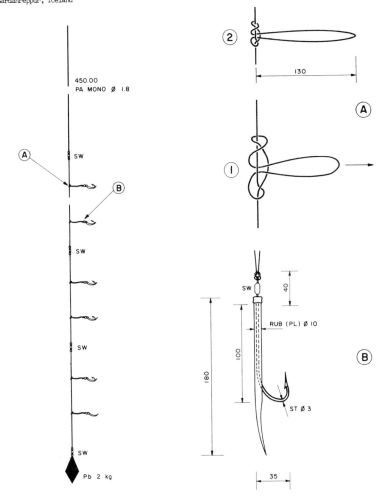

450.00
PA MONO Ø 1.8

SW

A

SW

B

SW

SW

SW
Pb 2 kg

② 130

A

①

SW

40

RUB (PL) Ø 10

100

180

B

ST Ø 3

35

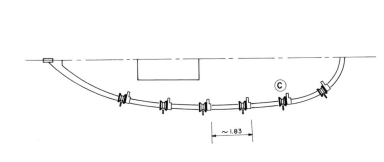

~1.83

C

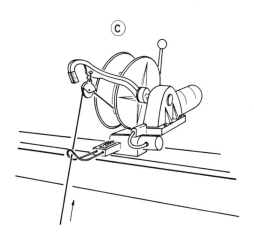

C

# LINES

Hand, with ripping hooks
With manual or electric reels
Squid
 I Day Fishing
II Night fishing (with light)
Japan

## REFERENCE

Ichiro Hayashi
Tokai Regional Fisheries Research Laboratory
5, Kachidoki, Chuoku, Tokyo, Japan

A.v. Brandt
Hamburg, Fed. Rep. of Germany

T. Mihara
FAO

# LIGNES

A main, avec turluttes
Avec moulinets manuels ou électriques
Encornet
 I Pêche de jour
II Pêche de nuit (avec la lumière)
Japon

# LINEAS

De mano, con añagazas
Con carreteles manuales o eléctricos
Calamar
 I Pesca de día
II Pesca de noche (con luces)
Japón

| VESSEL | BATEAU | BARCO | |
|---|---|---|---|
| Loa | Lht | Et | 9 - 10 m |
| GT | TJB | TB | 3 - 5 |
| hp | ch | cv | 35 |

50.00 - 200.00
PA MONO Ø 1.6
WIRE Ø 1

SW

x 30 - 40

PA MONO Ø 0.6 - 1

~ 2.50

PA MONO Ø 0.6 - 1

3.00 - 4.00

0.5 - 1 kg

50.00 - 200.00
PA MONO Ø 1.6
WIRE Ø 1

SW

~ 0.80

x 50 - 70

PA MONO Ø 0.6 - 1

3.00 - 4.00

0.5 - 1 kg

Pb 30 - 35 g

88

PL 25 - 30 g

RUB

95

+ ELEC MOT

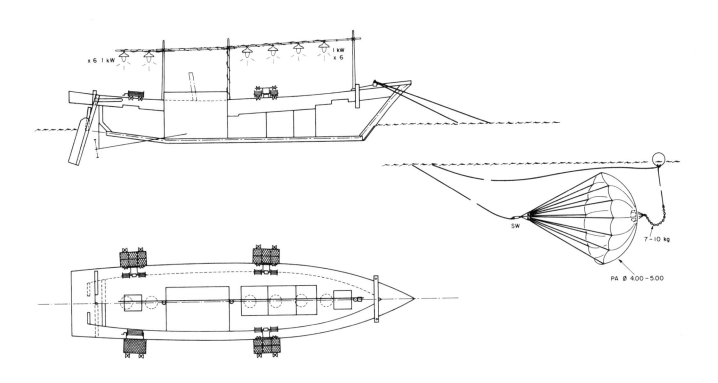

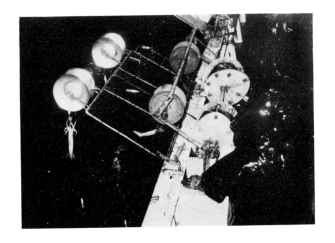

REFERENCE

A. Percier
Centre d'études et de recherches scientifiques
Biarritz, France

| VESSEL | BATEAU | BARCO | |
|--------|--------|-------|--------|
| Loa | Lht | Et | 10 - 15 |
| GT | TJB | TB | - |
| hp | ch | cv | - |

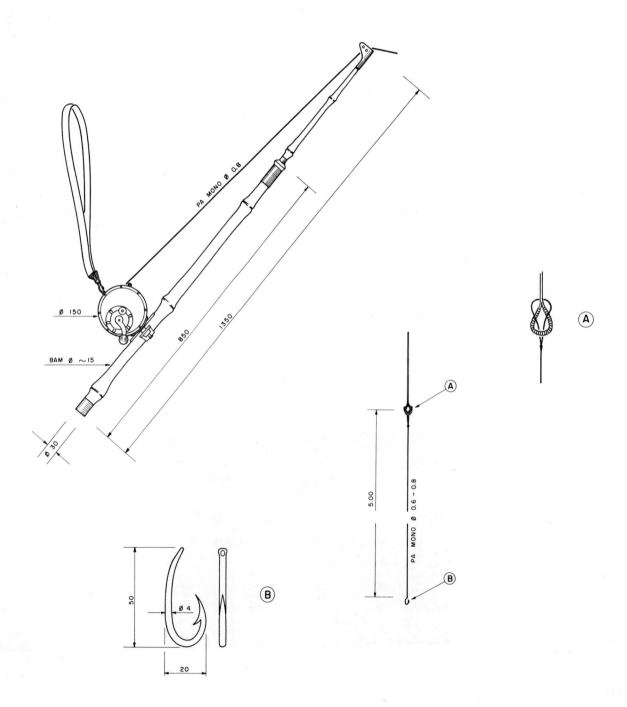

170

# LINES

Pole
Mackerel
Japan

# LIGNES

A la canne
Maquereau
Japon

# LINEAS

Con caña
Caballa
Japón

REFERENCE

T. Mihara
FAO

| VESSEL | BATEAU | BARCO | |
|--------|--------|-------|--------|
| Loa | Lht | Et | 8 - 15 m |
| GT | TJB | TB | - |
| hp | ch | cv | 10 - 50 |

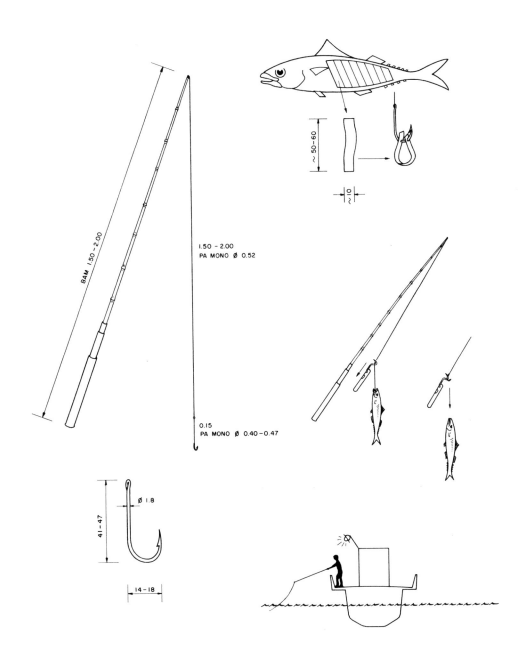

BAM 1.50 - 2.00

1.50 - 2.00
PA MONO Ø 0.52

0.15
PA MONO Ø 0.40 - 0.47

~ 50 - 60

Ø 1.8

41 - 47

14 - 18

171

# LINES

Pole, with live-bait
Tuna
Pacific, Fiji Islands
(see p. 98 for bait catching operation)

# LIGNES

A la canne, avec appât vivant
Thon
Pacifique, Iles Fidji
(Voir p. 98 pour la méthode de capture de l'appât)

# LINEAS

Con caña, con carnada viva
Atunes
Pacífico, Islas Fiji
(Véase pág. 98 método de captura de carnada)

## REFERENCE

R.M. Stone
Fisheries Division
Lami, Suva, Fiji

R. Lee
FAO

| VESSEL | BATEAU | BARCO | |
|--------|--------|-------|-------|
| Loa | Lht | Et | 15 m |
| GT | TJB | TB | - |
| hp | ch | cv | - |

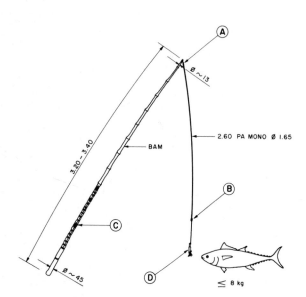

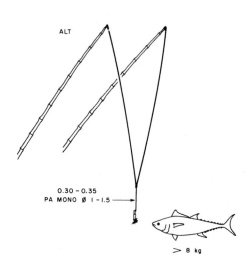

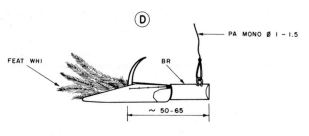

172

## LINES

Pole
With pearl-shell lure
Skipjack
Pacific, Tahiti

### REFERENCE

W. Reed, L. Devambez, J. Fyson
FAO

## LIGNES

A la canne
Avec leurre en nacre d'huître perlière
Listao
Pacifique, Tahiti

## LINEAS

Con caña
Con añagaza de nácar de concha
 perlera
Listado
Pacífico, Tahiti

| VESSEL | BATEAU | BARCO | |
|---|---|---|---|
| Loa | Lht | Et | 7 - 10 m |
| GT | TJB | TB | - |
| hp | ch | cv | 60 - 150 |

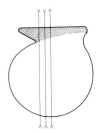

PRL SH CUT

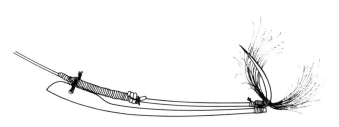

PEARL SHELL LURE

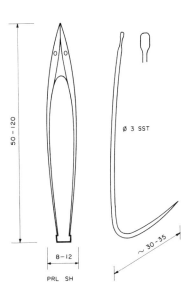

Ø 3 SST

50 - 120

8 - 12

PRL SH

~ 30 - 35

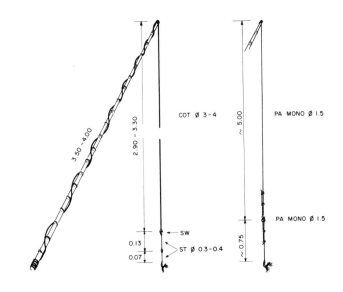

3.50 - 4.00

2.90 - 3.30

COT Ø 3 - 4

0.13
0.07

SW

ST Ø 0.3 - 0.4

~ 5.00

PA MONO Ø 1.5

~ 0.75

PA MONO Ø 1.5

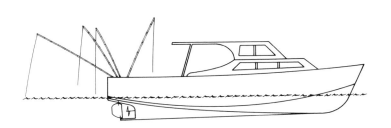

173

## LINES

Longline
Bottom set
Dogfishes, skates, conger, ling
English Channel, France

### REFERENCE

M. Giret
Valognes, France

## LIGNES

Palangre
De fond
Chiens, raies, congre, lingue
Manche, France

## LINEAS

Palangre
De fondo
Galludos, rayas, congrio, maruca
Canal de la Mancha, Francia

| VESSEL | BATEAU | BARCO | |
|--------|--------|-------|---------|
| Loa | Lht | Et | 14 – 15 m |
| GT | TJB | TB | 20 – 30 |
| hp | ch | cv | 150 |

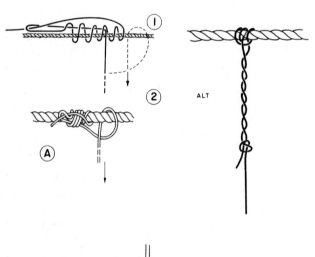

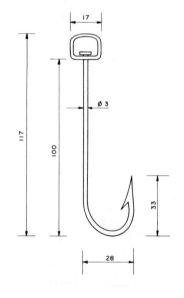

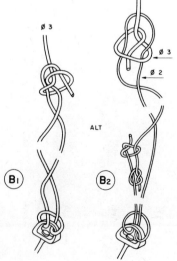

**174**

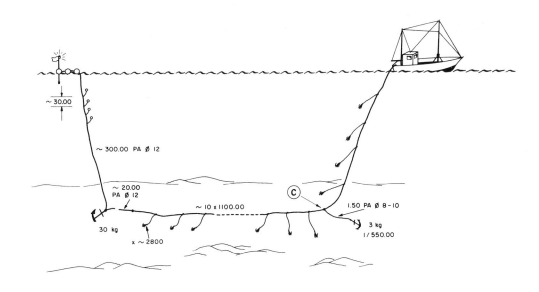

~ 30.00

~ 300.00 PA Ø 12

~ 20.00
PA Ø 12

30 kg

x ~ 2800

~ 10 x 1100.00

1.50 PA Ø 8-10

3 kg
1 / 550.00

Ⓒ

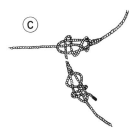

Ⓒ

# LINES

Longline
Bottom set
Sharks
Victoria, Australia

# LIGNES

Palangre
De fond
Requins
Victoria, Australie

# LINEAS

Palangre
De fondo
Tiburones
Victoria, Australia

REFERENCE

W.D. Hughes
Fisheries Division, Department of Primary Industry
Canberra, Australia

| VESSEL | BATEAU | BARCO | |
|--------|--------|-------|------|
| Loa | Lht | Et | 12 – 15 m |
| GT | TJB | TB | – |
| hp | ch | cv | 100 – 150 |

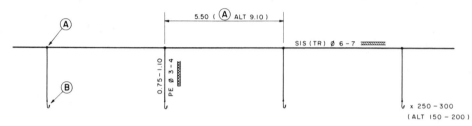

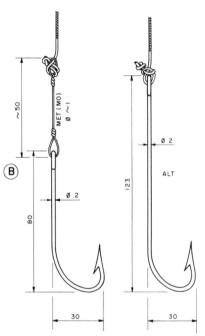

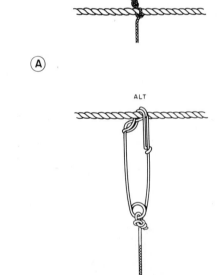

Ⓐ

ALT

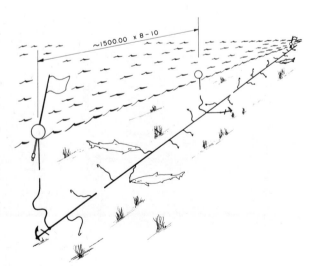

~1500.00  x 8 – 10

**176**

# LINES

Longline
Bottom set
Cod, haddock, ling
Westman Islands, Iceland

## REFERENCE

G. Jonasson
FAO

# LIGNES

Palangre
De fond
Morue, églefin, lingue
Iles Westman, Islande

# LINEAS

Palangre
De fondo
Bacalao, eglefino, maruca
Islas Westman, Islandia

| VESSEL | BATEAU | BARCO | |
|--------|--------|-------|------|
| Loa | Lht | Et | 11 m |
| GT | TJB | TB | 12 |
| hp | ch | cv | 64 |

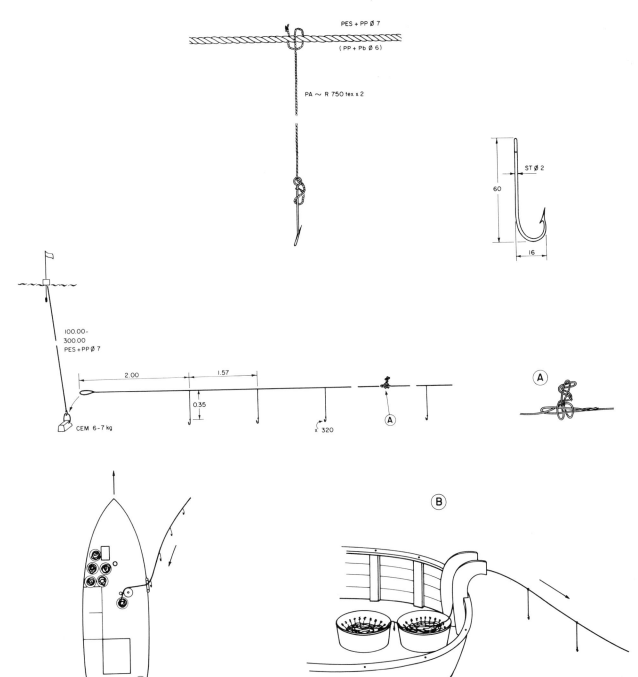

PES + PP Ø 7

( PP + Pb Ø 6)

PA ~ R 750 tex x 2

ST Ø 2

60

16

100.00-
300.00
PES + PP Ø 7

2.00

1.57

0.35

CEM 6-7 kg

x 320

A

B

# LINES

Longline
Bottom set
Catfish, red snapper
Gulf of Siam, Thailand

# LIGNES

Palangre
De fond
Poisson-chat, vivaneau
Golfe du Siam, Thaïlande

# LINEAS

Palangre
De fondo
Barbo, castañuela
Golfo de Siam, Tailandia

## REFERENCE

Somchart Sutchawongs
Marine Fisheries Station
Songkhla, Thailand

G. Jonasson
FAO

A.v. Brandt
Hamburg, Fed. Rep. of Germany

| VESSEL | BATEAU | BARCO | |
|--------|--------|-------|-----|
| Loa | Lht | Et | 6 m |
| GT | TJB | TB | – |
| hp | ch | cv | 7 |

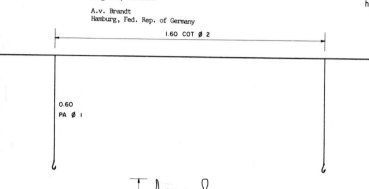

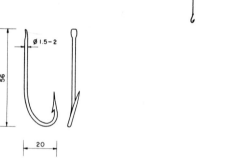

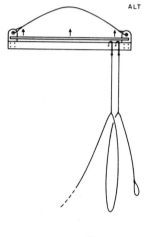

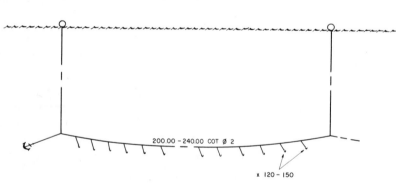

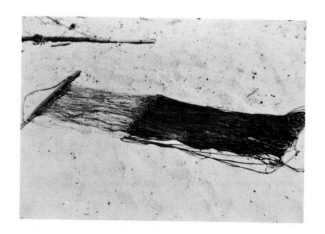

**178**

Longline
Bottom set, floating
Sea breams, grouper
Mediterranean, Libya

Palangre
De fond, flottante
Sparidés, mérous
Méditerranée, Libye

Palangre
De fondo, flotante
Espáridos, chernas
Mediterráneo, Libia

REFERENCE

A. Adragna
FAO

| VESSEL | BATEAU | BARCO | |
|--------|--------|-------|-------|
| Loa | Lht | Et | 6 – 8 m |
| GT | TJB | TB | – |
| hp | ch | cv | – |

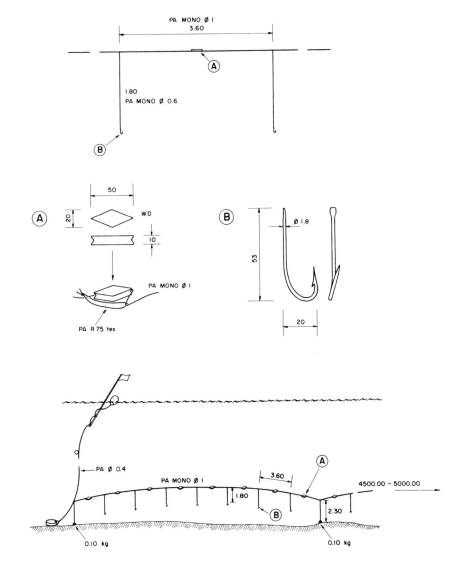

LINES

Longline
Bottom set, floating
Octopus
Rep. of Korea (East coast)

LIGNES

Palangre
De fond, flottante
Poulpe
Rép. de Corée (côte est)

LINEAS

Palangre
De fondo, flotante
Pulpo
Rep. de Corea (costa oriental)

REFERENCE

A.v. Brandt
Hamburg, Fed. Rep. of Germany

| VESSEL | BATEAU | BARCO | |
|--------|--------|-------|---|
| Loa | Lht | Et | 4 - 6 m |
| GT | TJB | TB | 1 |
| hp | ch | cv | - |

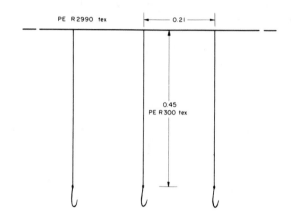

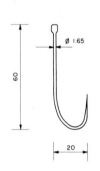

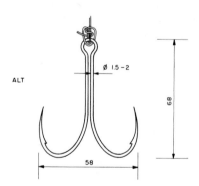

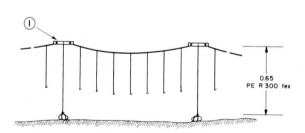

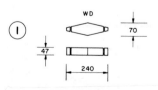

# LINES

Longline
Drifting
Swordfish
S. Tyrrhenian Sea, Strait of Sicily
Italy

## REFERENCE

G. Bombace
Laboratorio di Tecnologia della Pesca
Ancona, Italy

P. Arena
Centro Sperimentale Pesca
Messina, Italy

# LIGNES

Palangre
Dérivante
Espadon
Mer Tyrrhénienne, Détroit de Sicile
Italie

S. Thériault
FAO

# LINEAS

Palangre
De deriva
Pez espada
Mar Tirreno, Canal de Sicilia,
Italia

| VESSEL | BATEAU | BARCO | |
|--------|--------|-------|--------|
| Loa | Lht | Et | 13 - 15 m |
| GT | TJB | TB | 20 - 30 |
| hp | ch | cv | 80 - 150 |

PL Ø ~600

6000.00 - 12000.00

PL / RUB Ø ~100

PL / RUB Ø 300

~2.00

(B)

12.00

PA MONO Ø ~3

x 500 - 1000

(A)

70.00

5.00 PA MONO Ø 2

(A)

92

Ø 3

36

(B)

(C)

CK

300.00 - 400.00

(C)

# LINES

Longline
Drifting
Tuna
Taiwan , China

### REFERENCE

A.v. Brandt
Hamburg, Fed. Rep. of Germany

# LIGNES

Palangre
Dérivante
Thon
Taiwan , Chine

# LINEAS

Palangre
De deriva
Atunes
Taiwan , China

| VESSEL | BATEAU | BARCO | |
|--------|--------|-------|---------|
| Loa | Lht | Et | 14 – 15 m |
| GT | TJB | TB | 13 – 20 |
| hp | ch | cv | 30 – 60 |

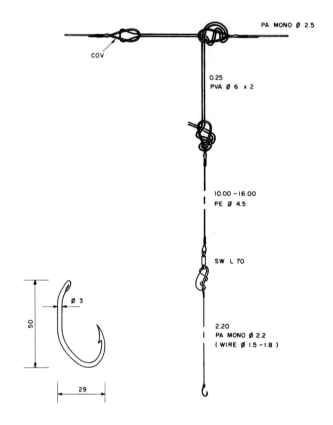

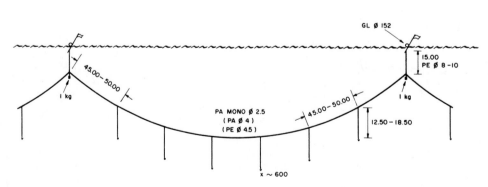

# LINES

Longline, vertical
Drifting
  I Yellowtail
    Japan
  II Red snapper
    Virgin Isl., Caribbean

### REFERENCE

  I  T. Mihara
     FAO

  II  D.A. Olsen, A.E. Damman, Don Neal
     (in Marine Fisheries Review, Jan. 1974)

# LIGNES

Palangre verticale
Dérivante
  I Sériole
    Japon
  II Vivaneau
  Iles Vierges, Caraïbes

# LINEAS

Palangre vertical
De deriva
  I Seriola
    Japón
  II Castañuela
  Islas Vírgenes, Caribe

| VESSEL | BATEAU | BARCO | I | II |
|--------|--------|-------|-----|-----|
| Loa | Lht | Et | 5 - 7 m | 6 m |
| GT | TJB | TB | - | - |
| hp | ch | cv | 10 - 17 | - |

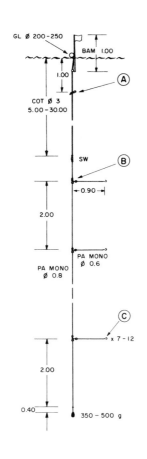

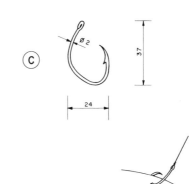

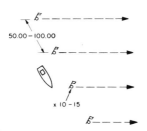

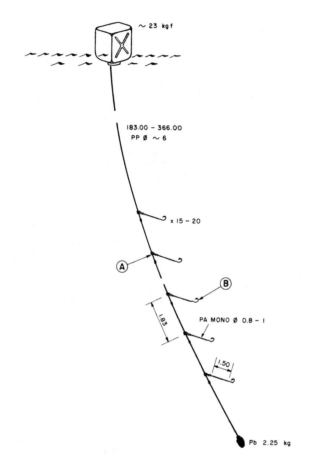

(II)

~ 23 kgf

183.00 – 366.00
PP Ø ~ 6

x 15 – 20

(A)

(B)

1.83

PA MONO Ø 0.8 – 1

1.50

Pb 2.25 kg

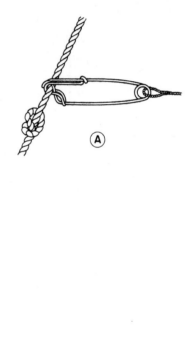

(A)

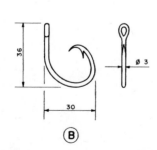

36

30

Ø 3

(B)

# LINES

Trolling
Surface
Little tunny, skipjack, yellowfin
New Caledonia

## REFERENCE

R. Criou, M. Legand
O.R.S.T.O.M.
Nouméa, Nouvelle-Calédonie

# LIGNES

De traîne
En surface
Thonnine, listao, albacore
Nouvelle-Calédonie

# LINEAS

Curricán
De superficie
Bacoreta, listado, rabil
Nueva Caledonia

| VESSEL | BATEAU | BARCO | |
|--------|--------|-------|--------|
| Loa | Lht | Et | 8 - 12 m |
| GT | TJB | TB | - |
| hp | ch | cv | - |

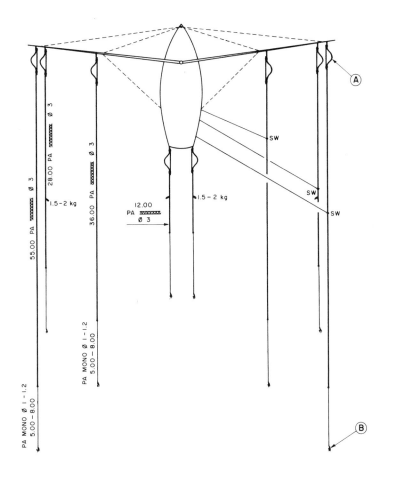

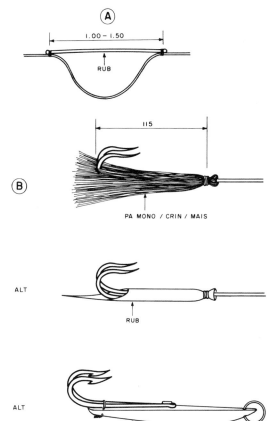

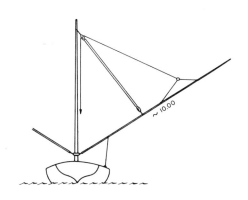

185

LINES

Trolling
 I Surface
II Diving
Albacore
New Zealand

LIGNES

De traîne
 I En surface
II Plongeantes
Germon
Nouvelle-Zélande

LINEAS

Curricán
 I De superficie
II Sumergidas
Albacora
Nueva Zelandia

### REFERENCE

 I N.F. Parsons
   Fishing Industry Board
   Wellington, New Zealand

II Loo Chi Hu
   Fisheries Research Division
   Ministry of Agriculture and Fisheries
   Wellington, New Zealand

| VESSEL | BATEAU | BARCO | I | II |
|--------|--------|-------|-----|-----|
| Loa | Lht | Et | 12 – 15 m | 6 – 8 m |
| GT | TJB | TB | – | – |
| hp | ch | cv | – | – |

12.00  Alu Ø 100

RUB Ø 460

PA MONO Ø 2-2.5

FAC

PA MONO Ø 2-2.5

PA MONO Ø 2-2.5

PA MONO Ø 2-2.5

PA XXXXX Ø 3-4

PA XXXXX Ø 3 - 4

Pb
~ 1.6 kg
FAC

SW

PA MONO Ø 1.6
~ 1.80

PA MONO Ø 1.6

PL
GRE

FEAT
WH

~ 69

~ 35

BR
CHRO

PL
RED

SW

**186**

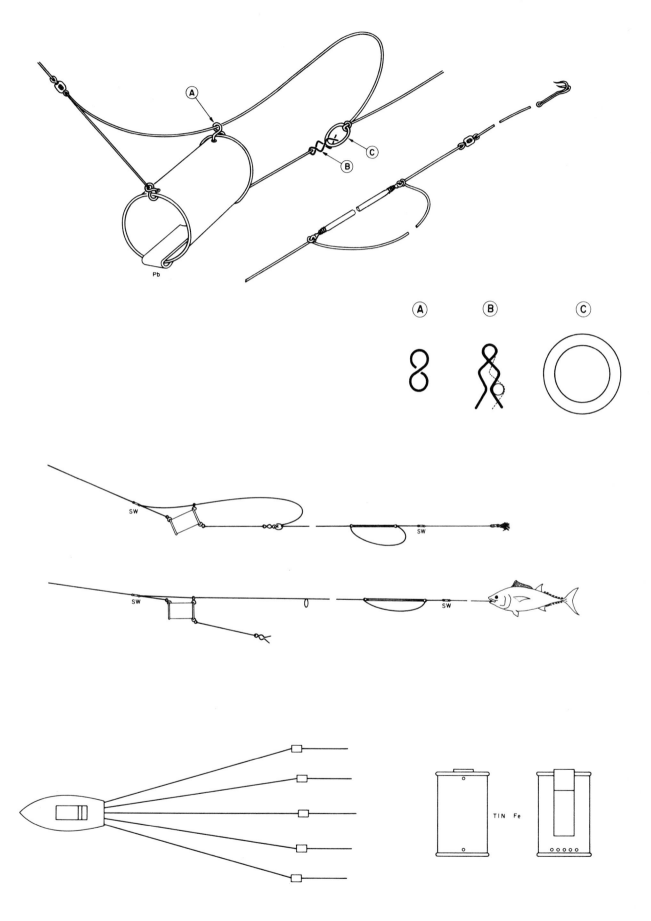

Hand-operated
Capelin
Saint-Pierre and Miquelon
North-West Atlantic

**HAVENEAU**
Manoeuvré à la main
Capelan
Saint-Pierre et Miquelon
Atlantique Nord-Ouest

**SALABARDO**
Maniobrada con la mano
Capelán
Saint-Pierre y Miquelón
Atlántico Noroeste

REFERENCE
B. Paturel
Institut des Pêches Maritimes
Saint-Pierre et Miquelon
Amérique du Nord

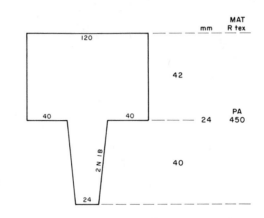

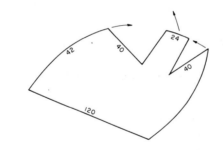

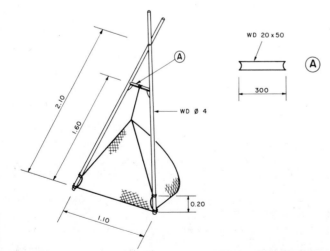

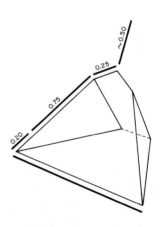

## SCOOP NET
Boat-operated
Freshwater fishes
Lake Chilwa, Malawi

## HAVENEAU
Manoeuvré du bateau
Poissons d'eau douce
Lac Chilwa, Malawi

## SALABARDO
Maniobrada desde el barco
Peces de agua dulce
Lago Chilwa, Malawi

REFERENCE

C. Ratcliffe
Ministry of Agriculture and Natural Resources
Zomba, Malawi

VESSEL BATEAU BARCO

| Loa | Lht | Et | 4-5 m |
|-----|-----|-----|-------|
| GT | TJB | TB | - |
| hp | ch | cv | 2-4 |

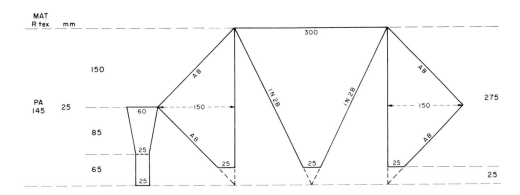

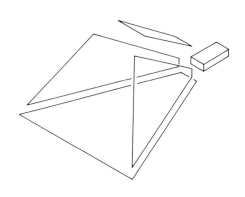

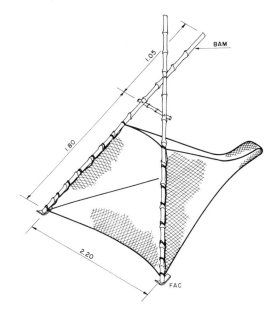

189

## SCOOP NET
"Lusenga"
Ndagala
Lake Tanganyika, Burundi

## HAVENEAU
"Lusenga"
Ndagala
Lac Tanganika, Burundi

## SALABARDO
"Lusenga"
Ndagala
Lago Tanganyika, Burundi

### REFERENCE
A. Collart, L. Haling, K.H. Hill
FAO

VESSEL  BATEAU  BARCO

| Loa | Lht | Et | 5-7 m |
|-----|-----|-----|-------|
| GT  | TJB | TB | -     |
| hp  | ch  | cv | -     |

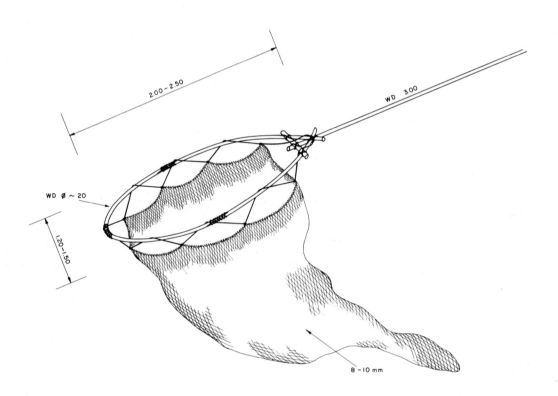

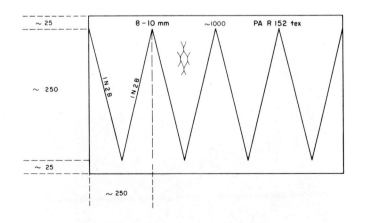

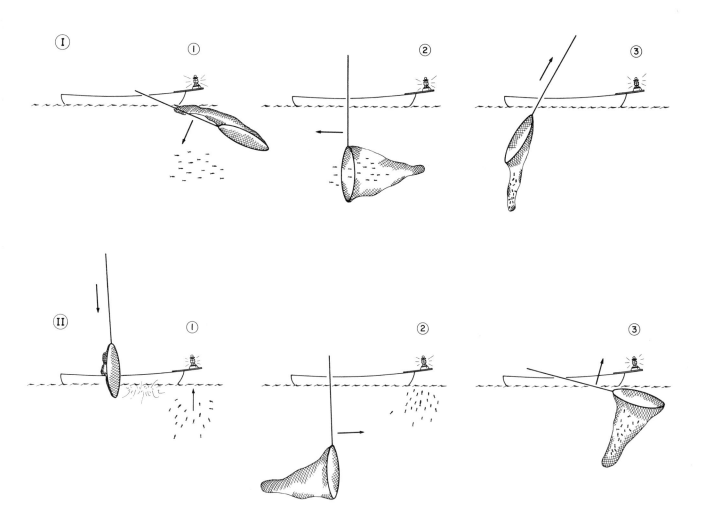